T0381041

AuthorHouse™
1663 Liberty Drive
Bloomington, IN 47403
www.authorhouse.com
Phone: 833-262-8899

ISBN: 978-1-6655-2391-2 (sc)
ISBN: 978-1-6655-2392-9 (e)

Library of Congress Control Number: 2021908464

Print information available on the last page.

Published by AuthorHouse 04/30/2021

authorHOUSE®

# *Scientific Doctor Science Practice*

*By: Scientist & Doctor Jaheem R.Hilts*

*1220 Scientific Society Founder*
*Commander & Chief Jaheem R.Hilts*
*Also he is, Scientific Doctor of Human*
*Evolution Doctor Jaheem R.Hilts*

*Historical*
*Schenectady, New York*

# Great Dedications
# The United States President's

1st George Washington
2nd John Adams
3rd Thomas Jefferson
4th James Madison
5th James Monroe
6th John Quincy Adams
7th Andrew Jackson
8th Martin Van Buren
9th William Henry Harrison
10th John Tyler
11th James K.Polk
12th Zachary Taylor
13th Millard Fillmore
14th Franklin Pierce
15th James Buchanan
16th Abraham Lincoln
17th Andrew Johnson
18th Ulysses S.Grant
19th Rutherford B.Hayes
20th James Garfield
21st Chester A.Arthur
22nd & 24th Grover Cleveland
23rd Benjamin Harrison
25th William McKinley
26th Theodore Roosevelt
27th William Howard Taft
28th Woodrow Wilson
29th Warren G.Harding

30<sup>th</sup> Calvin Coolidge
31<sup>st</sup> Herbert Hoover
32<sup>nd</sup> Franklin D. Roosevelt
33<sup>rd</sup> Harry S. Truman
34<sup>th</sup> Dwight D. Eisenhower
35<sup>th</sup> John F. Kennedy
36<sup>th</sup> Lyndon B. Johnson
37<sup>th</sup> Richard M. Nixon
38<sup>th</sup> Gerald R. Ford
39<sup>th</sup> James Carter
40<sup>th</sup> Ronald Reagan
41<sup>st</sup> George H.W. Bush &
Barbara P. Bush
42<sup>nd</sup> William J. Clinton
Hillary R. Clinton
43<sup>rd</sup> George W. Bush
44<sup>th</sup> Barack Obama
45<sup>th</sup> Donald J. Trump
46<sup>th</sup> Joseph R. Biden Jr.
-Love-

# -Love & in Memory-
## Of
# Mary N. Murdock

*February 18th, 1946-March 24th, 2016*

Author of:
Completion of a Heart: Love and The Mystics
The US Congressional Kid: Autobography 2009
The Four Masonic Children's Stories
The Journey of The Circle Whisperer
The Satanic Pope Enlightenment: Masonic Philosophy


Future Book coming soon..........
Illuminati God of The Female: Females Inspiration
By: Jaheem R.Hilts
-"Supporting The Female Species for Eternity"-

# Honorable Dedications

Donald Miller Lewis
Kevin Townley
Willy Harris
Lewis Hilts
Van Halen
Marilyn Manson
Ozzy Osbourne
Alice Cooper
Led Zeppelin
Justin Vos
Aleister Crowley
Anton Szandor LaVey
Satan Xerxes Carnacki LaVey
Zeena Schreck
Karla LaVey
Gladdice Sutton
Wilma Harris
Great Legend Artist and Entertainer DMX Earl Simmons
Mother-Yolanda E.Harris
Father-Jeffrey L.Hilts
Ellis Hospital Security Staff
Director of Operations @YMCA Edward J.Kowalczyk

Rap Artist King Von "Chicago"
Rap Artist Pop Smoke "Brooklyn"
Special Dedication to my Natural Sperm cell Father Jaheem R.Hilts
Publishing Consultant Derrick Austin of Author House
The Klansman & Illuminati Pope Bavaria Germany Jaheem R.Hilts
Publishing Coordinator of Author House Eve Ardell

American Red Cross
Blue Cross Blue Shield Association

Schenectady Police Department
531 Liberty St
Schenectady, NY 12305

The White House
1600 Pennsylvania Avenue NW,
Washington, DC 20500

Library of Congress
101 Independence Ave SE,
Washington, DC 20540

The Satanic Temple
64 Bridge St
Salem, MA 01970

The United States Army
The United States Marine Corps
The United States Navy
The United States Air Force
The United States Space Force
The United States Coast Guard

National Aeronautics and Space Administration NASA official:
Brian Dunbar

# Scientific Doctor Science Practice

Dec. 2nd, 2020

Doctor of Medicine
Awarded by
1220
Scientific Society

Awarded: Jaheem R.Hilts
Scientific Doctor=
Jaheem R.Hilts
Scientist= Jaheem R.Hilts

This is a Great achievement awarded to me Jaheem R.Hilts, in The Scientific Communtity of The 1220 Scientific Society. I am being awarded a Doctor of Medicine Degree. I believe as well as others my Scientific practices are as equivalent to practicing medicine in nature of Humanity. I more then desire to help The World in its course of Evolution, not just me- all of 1220 Scientific is a Help for people. [1220 Scientific Society Report]

# Table of Content

Chapters also translated into-Chinese, German, Spanish
About: West Coast Gang Counselor

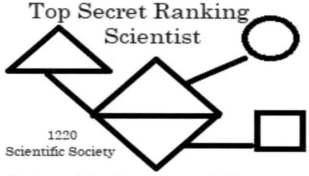

Top Secret Ranking
Scientist

1220
Scientific Society

Scientific Doctor of Human
Evolution Scientific Doctor=
Jaheem R.Hilts

(Certification)

I am a complete Scientist, I don't claim to be able to preform in duties I can't handle. Sometimes I'm just a helping hand, I wish to not disclose. I definitely specialize in Civilization, Research, Theory, Invention etc. As much is sensitive, there still is a need. I believe The World can have another Civilization without hurting The World Economy, Ethics, Time Zones or Evolution. There is much time wasted just existing in gravity hopeless, even hope can be misunderstood. I've reached more than my fair share of Secret Dimensions every little bit helps.

1220-Sci Report

*Life goes on. Weather brings trouble, we still make it throught. Love didn't leave me alone. Live to not speak in {Public}*

*1220 Sci-Soc report*

## SPIRITS OF THE CROWN
### ALL WOMAN'S SECRET SOCIETY #LROYALTY
### FOUNDER OF 1220 SCIENTIFIC SOCIETY

Founder of 1220- Jaheem R.Hilts
Royalty- Jaheem R.Hilts
Scientific Doctor- Jaheem R.Hilts
Doctor of Medicine- Jaheem R.Hilts

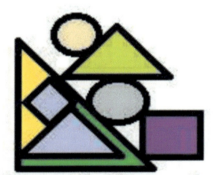

## Bone & Organisms Secret Society

1220
### Scientific Society
(Founder)

-King Illaminati- Jaheem R. Hilts-

*We are not a religious Secret Society. We don't tell what we are, rest assure we don't want ignorance to prosper within us. There is much to inherit before one is chosen to carry the Honor. We are backed by different Secret Societies 1st thing 1st don't worry don't tell.*

*1220 Sci-Society*

# Truthful Great Puba Mason
# Worshipful Majesty  Masonic

1220
Scientific Society
Founder

Scientific Doctor of Human Evolution
Doctor of Medicine
Jaheem R. Hilts

3-7-13-23

The truth will stay with the one chosen, never to be removed from the depth. Honor is like the time of infinity, parting is not real. To take on greatness is beyond the unbelief, the direction is Holy. Knowledge came first, then development took its course, without patience doom is subject to happen, like quick sand. Seekers are not looked for they find their way nothing is a obligation on The Worshipful its on The Seeker.

1220 Sci-Soc Report

## DINOSAUR BONE CHISEL
## SECRET SOCIETY
## 1220
SCIENTIFIC SOCIETY
1220 MEMBERS AND SCIENTIST
(SCIENTIST DOCTOR OF HUMAN EVOLUTION)
SCIENTIST- JAHEEM R. HILTS
1220 PRIVATE APPRENTICE

TWIST RESHAPE & STRUCTURE CORE BASICS. GIFT HONOR. LOSE CONSCIOUSNESS OF UNCONSCIOUSNESS SIGHT FOCUS. TRANSFORM THE IMPOSSIBLE. REMOVE OBSTACLES FROM ELEVATION. (TOP SECRET 1220)

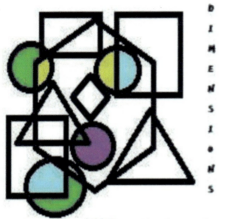

The Ultimate Sci-Fi level of

The 1220 Scientific Society

Scientific Doctor/Scientist of Human Evolution:

Scientist: Jaheem R.Hilts

This level is not designed to be achieved, as all of 1220 Scientific Society has blessed Secrets worth growing with and dying with. It's hard to deal with not expressing or talking from the Knowledge, Perception, and Initiation its better to avoid outsiders when you reach this level. It's simply intense very open minded. It's gradual it could even take years to inherit because determination and sincereity just doesn't mean I want everything. At this level a fool would want to speak it, what they are placed under, under meaning mental transition.

1220 Sci-Society

Founder

**FUTURE
PRESIDENTIAL CANDIDATE
JAHEEM R.HILTS**

The United States of America

1220
Scientific Society
Founder: Jaheem R.Hilts

Americans it's time to really take another look at how great your Country is. As a future candidate for Presidency of The United States of America, I will ensure you, I won't give up the fight to improve not just The Country but every American that stands with this Nation. We as people are supposed to help when we can, even me being elected I can't slack my duties to the people. Society has opportunities in it to satisfy the comfortability of all people. Don't condemn the system before looking at yourself and what you could have done to at least improve another fellow American. I want to work countless hours to bring this Nation to a higher standard for all levels of Citizens. We share this Country we should treat as our home not just in thought but in our respected actions. Nothing is guarnteed to be perfect working towards better in the direction of perfection may strike a mark where we don't have to move backwards but forward in our quest for a even greater Nation. I don't stand alone in this I stand with every individual Citizen. Be proud to be American make a difference as I seek to better America as your President Vote for Jaheem R.Hilts future US President.

# Earth must go on ......... (It Matters)

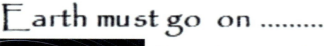

1220
Scientific Society
1220

Scientific Society
Founder:
Scientific Doctor= Jaheem R.Hilts

Everything happens with us as a World community, there is no burden too know each other, to know we are working together. Working around each other's irresponsibility in areas can help develop quicker, it doesn't mean it's necessary. Even the age of The Earth has not seen a (Future which has not seen a Future, which has not seen a Future). You can be mindless in love with Earth or -mindful-   1220 Sci-Soc

# Lincoln College of Technology

The Directors of the College on the recommendation of the College Faculty and by virtue of the Authority vested in them hereby Certify that

## Jaheem Rashon Hilts

has satisfactorily pursued the Studies and passed the Examinations and is therefore found worthy of graduation and entitled to receive this

## Diploma

### Welding Technology

with all the Rights, Privileges and Honors thereunto appertaining to this diploma.

March 28, 2018

Date Conferred

11194 E. 45th Avenue Denver Colorado 80239

_____
Campus President

_____
Academic Dean

# Jaheem R. Hilts
P.O.Box 630
Schenectady, NY 12305
(518) 844-4741

Jaheemjobs@gmail.com

***Objective: Seeking a position in the welding industry that will allow me to utilize my experience and education.***

## EDUCATION

Lincoln College of Technology       Denver, CO       Graduation: 3/28/18
- Welding Technology Diploma; learning proficiency in Stick, MIG, TIG welding process on Plate, and Pipe

Osha- 10 hour Construction Industry Course       July-2014

*Schenectady County Community College*       *January 2012-October 2014*
**Associates Degree in Applied Science in Alternative Energy Technology**

## WORK EXPERIENCE

**Free Lance**       **Boulder, CO**       **June 2016- September 2016**
- Picking weeds at recreational center  in the boulder area
- Built a fence at a religious organization
- Performed bee keeping for a religious organization
- Performed landscaping at various businesses in the Boulder Metro area

**Aspen Media**       **Boulder, CO**       **March 2015-May 2015**
*Interviewer*
- Contacted current customers to find out if they wanted to renew their subscriptions
- Contacted potential new customers based on leads passed by the company database

**Priceless Opportunities Real People Entertainment**  **Schenectady, NY**       **March 2013-October 2013**
*Owner*
- Video recorded weddings
- Helped small businesses create commercials
- Video recorded a concert for a religious organization
- Trained by Proctors Theater & SAG TV

**Wendy's Restaurant**       **Schenectady, NY**       **July-2012-July-2012**
*Service worker*
- Dish washer, food server, cook, food area janitor, food station janitor

**Corcraft**       **Alden, NY**       **November-2009- May-2010**
*Cleaning Operation:*
- *Ordered* inventory required for cleaning & maintenance duties
- Cleaned facility using chemicals and powered equipment
- Prepared cleaning solvents and solutions using given specifications
- Serviced, cleaned & supplied restrooms
- Sweep, mopped, scrubbed and vacuumed assigned floors
- Gathered and emptied trash

## VOLLUNTEER EXPERIENCE

- *Political campaign Activism 2014*       Boulder, CO       October-November 2014
  - 21,039 phone calls in a month
- *Political Campaign Activism 2016*       Longmont, CO       September-November 2016
  - Honk and wave signs to encourage voting
  - Poll watching
  - Handed out 3000 rally Yard signs at a political rally in Colorado Springs

# Early Origins of the Hilts family

The surname Hilts was first found in Bavaria, where the name was anciently associated with the tribal conflicts of the area. They declared allegiances to many nobles and princes of early history, lending their influence in struggles for power and status within the region. They branched into many houses, and their contributions were sought by many leaders in their search for power.

# Certificate of DNA Origins

*This certifies that on November 26, 2019*

# JAHEEM HILTS

*has undergone DNA testing to determine genetic ancestry.*

## Biogeographical Ancestry Results

| Estimate | Ancestry |
|----------|----------|
| 85% | Sub-Saharan African [AF] |
| 12% | European [EU] |
| 2% | Indigenous American [IA] |
| 1% | East Asian [EA] |

## Bar Graph of Results

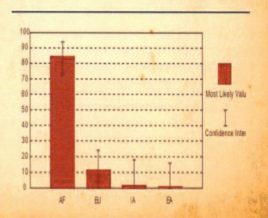

DNA ORIGINS

Case Number: 8714632    Report Date: 11/26/19

❖ *A Story about working out and weight training….*

*I don't know how to begin to explain; I will try to start where it can make sense, and be beneficial. I'm going to start where I was working out on and off since 15 yrs old. When I got 22 yrs old, I was working out harder. I would pay attention to what I eat. I loved the protein from Tuna in a can with Hot Sauce and no Mayo. Doing The Pull-Up Bar was of necessary when I worked out, I got up to 30 reps each set. When it comes to pull-ups sometimes you can do more, sometimes you go back to doing less. I started hitting weights on a routine which built core strength, no matter how you did it. I worked out with this routine from 2010 to current. I'm not going to say "I work out every day", but I will say "I will never stop working out". [Photo on next page of workout routine]*

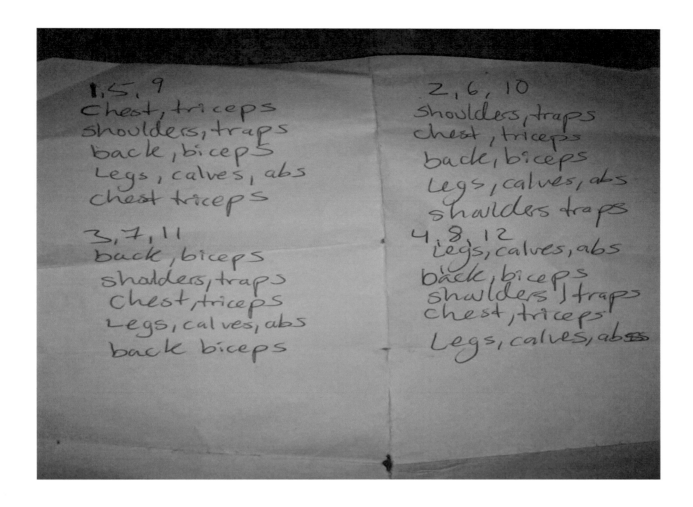

1, 5, 9
Chest, triceps
shoulders, traps
back, biceps
Legs, calves, abs
chest triceps

3, 7, 11
back, biceps
sholders, traps
Chest, triceps
Legs, calves, abs
back biceps

2, 6, 10
shoulders, traps
chest, triceps
back, biceps
Legs, calves, abs
shoulders traps

4, 8, 12
Legs, calves, abs
back, biceps
shoulders, traps
chest, triceps
Legs, calves, abs

Working out to me is fun, it clears my mind enriches my body and I have a goal to bring out these muscles. I have experience as a weight lifting trainer. One day I was working out and this guy Jesse, we went to the same school, he wanted to get down with my work out routine. I trained with Jesse for a little while once he grasped the routine he took it serious, he would do it on his own. Jesse blew himself up extra strong; he was like the small version of The Hulk. It made me feel good. I was known as the one that can transform people into their desire from showing them how to work out. While I was in College for a few Semesters, I was going to The YMCA through College tuition, training my Barber in weight lifting. We use to meet at The YMCA 5:00am every morning.

*My opportunity to be around Great Men started way before this. I never took it for granted, that's why I came so far in life. I would have died not revealing this picture or speaking about it. Since times are different I'm showing the picture not speaking about it....*

*{Scientist- Jaheem R.Hilts Bavaria Illuminati Member}*

    *Speaking about working out with The President of The College. I ran for Senior Senate of Student Government, in 11 minutes, and got more signatures than people who were running for months. This was in 2012-2013; I was also The Vice President of The Spanish Club. I would have been The President of The Spanish Club, if I was a few days early, in showing up.*

In life self advancement is priority. When one has no means of learning they live and exist with no hope or hope with no future. Emotions are not supposed to be taken as a form of reality when that is all people can thrive off. What would life be like if people didn't add to productivity or build more for Humanity. I lost myself in the right Knowledge that didn't seem to be fulfilled until time moved in more experience and comprehension became developed higher because understanding out weighed ignorance even when I knew everything that didn't make me ignorant.
1220° Scientific Society Founder Commander and Chief Jaheem R.Hilts
            Sci-Soc report(2021).................

1220° Scientific Society
Founder Jaheem R.Hilts

The constant burst of energy, hidden, then transformed into a endless rupture, creates a form of illumination and solid. Advancement into a flow unrecognized not sought by a endless number. Accusations are under scored within the understanding of the whole. Evolution is not based on repeat of existing. Finding comfort in natural existence aware of nature limitless calculated. High reflections and low reflections minimizing awareness so vast The Earth remains perfect.

(1220° Sci-Soc report)

## 1220° Scientific Society
### Founder

This World is beyond the comprehension of complexity. The lack of realization plays a major part in the advanced development of opportunity. Not just is it a consequence to be aware with no understanding, its a obstacle because it creates closed mindedness. I try to provide a new way of looking at things. I know the tools to get to the point one is stuck in study, its a priceless treasure. Why is real questioned? Why is fake accepted & noticed at the same time? What does the future hold? Why judge? Why not judge? What to let go? What's worth holding on to?

Leading Scientist of 1220° Jaheem R.Hilts

1220° Scientific Society Founder
Scientific Doctor-Jaheem R.Hilts

People are use to being blind by their behavior which is a unnoticed habit. The things they do are not wrong in their eyes when they can suffer any level of consequence. Their memory is based off acceptance instead of (xyz). There is a major battle in people which is not seen commonly or rarely. This battle is not realized without awareness. Even consciousness is questioned, where does The World go¿ I am a Scientist with less interest in (xyz). I have never failed myself and only came short to a false perception rather than a Honest perception.

1220° Sci-Soc report 2021

I feel like people would get farther in life, if they told the truth instead of lying, leaving that experience of not being able to trust a person, on the mind of others. It's a shame how something's are with held because of no interest, then its another thing how things are with held because of past situations, of experiencing untrustworthiness. Usually dealing with people, I've learned, telling the truth builds trust, so if a lot of people wanted trust to be a wave or something big in the world, they would get trust by telling the truth.
1220° Scientist Jaheem R.Hilts

In this World we have to over come what we think we know, and understand what it is to exist in Reality, instead of making up our own. There lays a heavy disaster when we are locked in ignorance, then that builds to be the only thing happening. The World is beyond Religion alone, and we can't take away from The Religious values, because it helps us build into Honorable people, if we choose to be. In fact people need to grow into a better them first, then add on to what relationships they have with people, sometimes that's looked past because doing nothing seems pleasant when we can do more. The best is The best The great is The great.... These are words from 1220° Scientific Society Founder Scientist Jaheem R.Hilts 1986.

1220° Scientific Society Founder
Commander and Chief
The Satanic Pope Jaheem R.Hilts

I am a misunderstood & mistaken
Scientist, just like The Discovery & The
Development of things, from Evolution to
Awareness. Appreciating how The Key 🔑
to Greatness can't fit the lock to its
assigned unit, in the hands of one not
willing to use it. Finding out the
mechanisms to that, put me further in
study. Because I'm misunderstood and
people mistaken me, I didn't want nothing
to do with that. The Temperature with its
formation, can't be a act off delusion.

*Boulder Colorado*
*The Creek*
*College Vacation from Schenectady New York 2014-2021*

*I went to Colorado to graduate as a Wind Power Technology major. I graduated from College in Denver with a Welding Technology degree. Before I left Colorado I was mastering Science and became a Top Secret Scientist with my own Scientific Society called "1220 Scientific Society" I am The Founder Jaheem R.Hilts.*

# Chapter #1
# Come to realization....

Since it's a time in The World, where people are in a stage of blindness creating problems within themselves; out of themselves its best for me to explain how my Scientific Practices are equivalent to a Doctor of Medicine Degree. A Doctor of Medicine Degree is the highest Degree one can reach as a Doctor. Why would I choose to write on "Come to realization"? Here is my major point:

If we look at The World it's moving forward at a standstill. People are caught up in their daily activities and settling for things they do even when they are not doing anything. Come to realization by becoming open minded for starters. Getting in the groove of positivity, which has always been pleasant especially in the growth of the future. Destruction alone is chaos a point where there is no major growth and people are stuck oppressing each other not getting ahead at all. Coming to realization takes the everyday burden off the mind, body, and soul; happiness is easier to reach. A person must want well for themselves, to see results in change. Come to realization must bring change in the individual's life that comes to. Right here I'm going to present a quote to the audience of this book:

"Change is the most feared concept known to man".

I learned this from this man just travelling in this World still mingling with people, searching for knowledge. If you can identify with a problem in your life, you can change it or leave it. We all know we live in a World not ready to accept other things other people don't agree with. That shouldn't stop us as individuals. It should make us or the individual come to the realization and strive to bring about what needs to happen. That's why I don't support racism. I support Females and not Males. I just would never support them over Females.

# Chapter #2
# Why I shouldn't give up....

Why people shouldn't give up, not just is it failure and a negative memory, but it holds that person in a state of doubt. Yes we can learn from our trials and errors. We can learn from our mistakes. Why I shouldn't give up referring to the individual, something all people should be able to adjust to.

"Life is beautiful and you should know you matter".

There are different reasons why a person would matter. We would assume that people give themselves self worth; we know people should automatically love themselves. Another reason is how The World is going, not everybody, but there are people who add things to The World, that help other people on a massive level they more than matter. We can name a few things that came in handy for Humanity: The invention of toilet paper, protecting ones feet by inventing shoes. People do matter even if they don't want to accept it. Another reason why people should know they matter, because when you don't love yourself somebody else out there loves; cares about you. You matter by adding something to The World, because you love yourself or simply someone else loving you. That's a brief on why you or I shouldn't give up.

# Chapter #3
# What is healthy?

Things that are healthy, we can use exercise being the first one, getting proper rest being the second one. Then you have the way you manage your body & how you interact with people. If we look at health on the level we should, if we are healthy we would help another person get healthy or maintain their health. Spreading good vibes is healthy. Not being to prideful in cleaning up somebody else's mess is healthy. The reason I say these things is to help people open up a new part of their minds, and make their capabilities not hindered from false judgment, resistance, or just not caring about being healthy. When a person can think and know what is right, having it applied in their lives is a great health. There is a lot of junk in the brains of people and it spreads daily, overnight in the matter of seconds. A form of health would be to get rid of that stuff become more into *yourself and be a part of making The Planet Healthy.*

# Chapter #4
# How to get out of wanting to commit suicide

Suicide is a major topic for me to touch on. It's something I feel happy about, expressing my concerns about. I want it to be known, I have two or more incidents where I helped a person, come to the realization, which suicide wasn't for them. Along time ago probably in year 2009, I was around a guy facing 25 yrs to life. I don't remember his charges, but he was scared of prison. He told me countless times, when he got to prison he was going to hang himself. His reasons for wanting to hang himself, was he didn't know what jail was like. For weeks he would say "He was going to kill himself, he was going to kill himself", constantly over; over daily. I would speak good things to him and let him know, even though he would be in jail, his Mother needed him. In the beginning, he would not accept he needs to live. Then one day with a big smile on his face, he told me "He wasn't going to kill himself". When he said it to me, he just said it and walked away. He didn't even say anything after. I felt accomplished then I knew he was free. He was free from his mind being over taken; by he needs to end it. That's unnecessary pressure to go through. After a while in the same day, I and he talked; he would share with me, his Mother is going to send him packages; money, so he was happy about that. This was my biggest experience in helping somebody out of committing suicide. I shouldn't say "This is my biggest experience", because anytime you stop somebody from committing suicide, it's big. My next experience in helping suicide prevention was in Colorado. In Boulder Colorado, a homeless guy was behind a dumpster, in the freezing cold, he was an old man; he said "He wants to die behind there, nobody cares about him". Actually I did care about him. I'm a Mason, so I care about people, even if they don't know. After talking to him for a while, I asked him "Can I call the ambulance for him". He agreed he was cold, and wanted to be warm. He was freezing cold and would urinate on himself, just to stay warm. I called the ambulance and they came and took him away. I felt so good I saved another life. I remembered the first time. I don't think people, who haven't had the chance, to save a life like that, knew how it would feel. It's amazing, I even tried to take it a step further and do it as a career. Then I was slapped in the face, because it says "You need a Master's Degree to be a Suicide Prevention Counselor". I knew I didn't need a degree at all, because I helped people, come out of wanting to go through with it. The way to stop, yourself, from committing suicide is to look at life, not to give up. Mind over matter, talk to people, know you're not alone in The World. Don't shame yourself; try to sleep it off in the worst case scenario. I wish I was an actual, Suicide Prevention Counselor, where I can be on 24hr call, just to show another way, instead of taking your own life.

1220 Scientific Society Founder Commander & Chief
Scientific Doctor of Human Evolution Jaheem R.Hilts

# Chapter #5
# Why Hygiene is important?

As a Doctor, trying to get my understanding through to people, I may have to say things people already know, and at the same time I'm using Scientific Practices. The reason why hygiene is important is because poor hygiene can cause major problems, to the human body. Under close study the way to prevent most common reactions to outbreaks is cleanliness. Hygiene is important to reduce the foul odor smell the body might let out, when it's not taken care of. If people didn't pay attention to hygiene, it would cause a percentage of The World's population to affect, the other percentages of people who do. Most people can play in dirt and not have a negative reaction as long as they clean themselves properly. Not to get too involved in letting The Secrets out of my

Scientific Society, people need to figure out every method that will cleanse them and not cause a negative reaction, to the chemicals in the solutions or care products. People are in The State of Evolution, which means picking up the slack on hygiene; making sure it's a priority rather than an option.

# Chapter #6
# My last encounter with Mental Health and my scientific reasons to help

My last encounter with Mental Health was brutal but let me start by saying:

When I was 7 years old turning 8 years old, I fell out a two story window in Albany N.Y, on Trinity St 1994. I use to scare my Mother by telling her I was going to kill myself, so I was put into Mental Health. As I got older I dealt with Mental Health talking to Counselors and Specialists on issues. So basically I've been dealing with them off and on until 2021. I tried to go under evaluations to prove whatever it said when I was young was false, they wouldn't let me do that. For some strange reason you can never get a Mental Health record erased. I've tried doing this multiple times, which false accusations hinder me in a lot of areas especially that mental health paper trail. I could get my record sealed and expunged but I can't get my Mental Health record erased that's strange. My last encounter with them was abuse on their part to me. I was in the snow for hours I decided to go to The Hospital and get checked out for back pain; possible frost bite. I stayed overnight, made sure my phone was charged. In the morning I asked them "If I could get a ride in The Ambulance to State St and Hulett in Schenectady, N.Y". They said "Wait a moment" when they came back, they told me to "Sit in a chair", then wheeled me to a different room. I started fighting with the, telling the "I won't take my clothes off or give them my phone". We did that for a long time, and then they said "Either way I had to take a shot. I eventually let them give me the shot. Just to show them there was nothing wrong with me. I woke up in scrubs. The Security lady was nice enough to fill out a form, saying "It wasn't a threat to myself or other people, me having my earrings; rings on my fingers". So they didn't bother me about that. I tested negative for The Coronavirus, so I eventually got moved to Non-Coronavirus Unit. I was there doing normal stuff, I had to notify Social Security as well as The Federal Courthouse Northern District Albany, N.Y- that my rights were being violated, so they were aware. I was meeting with a Doctor who would just say "I need medication" because I get angry at him talking down to me or trying to make me stay in The Hospital. I became very defiant very disobedient. I broke windows with punches threw things all over. This was not because of my Mental State, this was because they tried to mess my life up, with a fake diagnosis and not doing a proper evaluation. I even told my Publishing Company Author House, "To update my account to Celebrity Author". I asked "Them to look up my books". I told them "I never did anything for them to have me in here". I told them "I was a Scientist with my own Scientific Society, I'm not crazy, the way I am is because I look at The World different". None of this worked, so I told one of The Staff "The same way I was breaking stuff, if they didn't let me out, I'm going to jail, beating the hell out one of them". They tried to make me take medication before they said "I was getting a second evaluation by The Head Psychiatrist there". I refused they tried to say "Then I can't speak to him". Long story short they said "Sit for an hour", then I talked to him and they let me out. I did put fifty million dollar lawsuit against them, and I didn't win but they got the point. I think I can do more for The Planet; people, then Mental Health can do, with my Scientific Practices, and like I said "I wasn't supposed to be placed in that situation". As a Scientist Doctor of Human Evolution, Mental Health is a very young Organization, Which "Yes" its treatments does help people. Then you have the taking advantage of people because of what I went through. I know I could help treat people without medication. I'm a Top Secret

*Scientist; I can't reveal dimensions or my Theories or Methods of Practice. It's either you understand, I know what I'm talking about or it's like a dead end, because I can't help at that point.*

# Chapter #7
# Rapist needs help

So a Doctor I can't bash the people I feel go against all ethics of living. The morals of a rapist, is messed up. Rapists have done more wrong to a Female than anything in The world. "Rapist needs help" needs to go into effect global. There is no need to rape a Female; because I'm a Scientist I've done much work and study on rapist. I know their motives and why they rape. I don't understand why they would choose to do it, but I understand. A rapist no matter how you look at it needs help. They need to be treated and or punished for their crimes against Females. The reason, why, I say "Females" because it happens to Females, of all ages, in my studies a man would plot against a Female for sexual pleasures, because he feels dominate & classifies a Female as weakness. They use their strength or luring a Female with ulterior motives, through manipulation. A rapist can rape as a sign of consequence, feeling like they were done wrong. A rapist needs help because they don't think about the trauma they put on a Female, let alone they don't understand a Female has the right to say "No". If a rapist becomes a rapist by learned behavior, they need to seek professional help, and never rape again. This has been going on for so long it needs to be treated it needs to be addressed and it needs to stop. Rapists aren't scared to rape because the consequences are not heavy enough on them, after defiling a Female. I didn't research the programs they have for rapist, but I know if the punishment doesn't become more severe, than this maybe a serious threat to a lot of Females. Not just to say "We need to put an end to sex trafficking because that's rape".

*The Scientific Doctor of Medicine. The God of The Female holding, "Completion of a Heart: Love and The Mystics".*

The Satanic Pope Jaheem R.Hilts 1220 Scientific Society

# Chapter #8
# Can meditation help me?

People already know music is a form of medicine. It usually touches the soul and entertains people. It's big in The World right now, so people can enjoy it. This chapter is not about music it's about meditation. Can meditation help me? Let me speak about meditation from me view point and how it can help somebody. I've been doing meditations for over a decade Secret meditations that transform the consciousness into center. Meditation can reset a mind that is off track. I didn't say it was something that will happen after the first meditation. I never gave up meditating so I've seen more than the results from doing it. When you look at yourself, it's hard to understand that you need to be more *humble or you need to take a step back, especially in the heat of the moment. When you look towards meditation to help you through the day, you change your concept and different energy you're dealing with. The meditations I conduct with other people it's guided by me. I guide people through solid meditations. I have received great comments on the benefits people got using my way of meditating, so I'm speaking on "Can meditation help me". In fact know that I'm speaking from a more developed understanding. As a Scientist get involved with meditation, no matter if you just do it for a little while. I can't understand how a person wouldn't love meditation but I understand everybody might not understand why they should do it. Just throwing it out there you use your brain to think, sometimes you may not feel like you're unsettled but if you get into meditation, all that might change and you will be handling your everyday self differently.*

# Chapter #9
# Another way to look at anger

As I begin to break this down I know people will probably think "I heard it all before". I would say "Really", anger this is another way to look at it. Anger spoils the fun it spoils all good vibes and can overpower all the other emotions. I believe all emotions should be recognized and under the control of the individual. Anger comes and goes even the angriest person in The World loves to be relaxed if they can. If we can break anger down from a Scientific point of view it is a balance. It's a mechanism classified as an emotion that alerts a person of a deeper disagreement. It's a form of rejection to something that occurred. It was never documented or told a person was angry for no reason. Like I said "The best way to deal with anger" is not to act on it. Let it come and go because nobody can say I'm never going to get angry. They can count on when I get angry, how I'm going to handle it. If you pay attention to what was said in this chapter you can see clearly, another way to look at it.

# Chapter #10
## I'm not a Medical Doctor I'm a Scientific Doctor

My reason for writing this book is to prove I have what it takes without medical school. My Scientific Practices are equivalent to a Doctor of Medicine Degree. I'm not a Medical Doctor I'm a Scientific Doctor of Human Evolution. There are multiple problems with Humanity I'm addressing Humans to be in fact. Since I took my studies serious as a Scientist I couldn't help to go all the way. I'm a Top Secret Scientist I specialize in many different areas of Science. I would probably be one of The Ultimate Medical Doctors if I studied that way of going. Let me let it be known I appreciate good Doctors who work in The Hospital performing medical duties from surgeries to check ups. What I have to bring to the table is beyond that. Everybody in The World doesn't listen to good news, what will help them, etc. That doesn't mean they are not aware. I will say most issues can be solved and The Planet can be on its course in a different direction more beneficial for Humanity. I take my Scientific Practices serious so I don't disclose them. What I do is provide knowledge and information prominent to help other people in my journey. I wouldn't be able to just walk around talking about it if I wasn't about it. I see things deeper than a microscope. I know I'm elite whether people accept it or not. I didn't just waste my time going on 14 years in Secret Societies for nothing. I figured it out so I wasn't lost or stuck in a World where nobody knew counting on old knowledge and information to get them by. I can't reveal any way I built people building myself and in a new beginning I have my own Scientific Society waiting to conduct Top Secret

Operations to help in The World that are not harmful to humans. 1220 Scientific Society I'm Commander and Chief all practices are sensitive so it's just me on the outside looking in. I reached a level that made me one and million in all Scientific Society communities with 7 billion people in The World only 700,000 people have the potential. They could be dead or alive to be exact. Especially as a Scientist majority of the people in The World is closed minded, they don't even want to learn then continue they rather pass up the opportunity. Not just to say 1220 Scientific Society has 80 years to reign from 2020 to 2100. That's a blessing I want to make a lot of good research & documentation happen in that time. I had a few people on the waiting list just to know what 1220 meant and it turned out they didn't make the cut. So I didn't lost anything and I know 1220 is still protected.

# Chapter #11
## Don't die from an overdose

Just because I'm a Doctor & a Scientist with my own Scientific Society, doesn't mean I don't understand. Growing up, I use to look down on certain drugs. When I got older I experienced some and more drugs I would have never did. I went to Colorado on a College vacation from Schenectady, N.Y. Before I left New York the only drugs I used was Marijuana, Ecstasy, Molly, Acid, and Alcohol. When I got to Colorado not shortly after Cocaine was free. I didn't get it all the time but when I did it was usually to party. To sum it up quick, in Colorado I use Cocaine, Meth, Crack, Mushrooms etc if I can't remember. I wasn't a pill popper like that and stayed away from Heroine. The reason why I explained what I did is because I want people who use to understand I'm not just talk. I never considered myself an addict because I did drugs to experience the high; I didn't do drugs because I needed to be high. I wouldn't jeopardize anything important behind using drugs. As a Scientist drugs are not important yes they break up homes, ruin lives, sometimes bring people together, but don't die from an overdose. If I can't stop people from using drugs, please use in moderation. Don't die from an overdose. One time I almost overdosed on Molly. I was doing three grams and a few days after I started, I took an expanded amount from water. I swear if I wouldn't have thrown up the water I would have been dead. I was high for the next three days. It didn't matter if I fell asleep I would wake up high. If you can seek help on how to stop using drugs or at least be safe using them, you will be better off.

# Chapter #12
# Understand your body

As people sometimes we take life for granted. I use to be a part of "As people" that's why I said that. Now with my knowledge from researching and studying I learned more. I'm aware of the harm I would put myself in by not understanding your body. So understand your body is geared towards the reading audience & people in general. Now saying "Understand your body" paying attention to specifics, you have to worry about every element of your human existence. Not getting the proper rest can affect how you operate in the future. I want to speak about how the body is working and how to keep it working. Over the course of time you hear things about boosting your immune system. Hearing that so much you think there is nothing else to boost yes there is. I maybe writing a Doctor practice providing topics and necessary information but I'm going to leave it open for you to do further research. Of course there are other things to boost in the human body which will allow you to understand your body. It's common for people to wait on a check up or feeling some type of pain to go see a Doctor. They are not professionals, going to see professionals for their issues, or they maybe professionals. Even a Doctor will go see a Doctor. It's time to understand your body, find out what's happening with you. If you know about yourself keep doing more research. Make sure you can identify with your breathing on a more concrete level not just being conscious of breathing. Don't fail yourself understand your body.

# Chapter #13
# How to take care of myself and how to treat others

Since I'm talking about how to take care of myself, I have to say "I have to do a good job". I'm a Scientific Doctor of Human Evolution; I'm dealing with this World on a different level. It's not just essential for me to make sure I'm clean & got food to eat. I basically have to continue to study and research so I'm not in darkness mentally. Since I was younger a right & exact Mason, I knew I had to keep going with my studies. Being a Mason has nothing to do with trying to bring people in or giving away The Secret Knowledge. I'm over happy I'm a Mason. Taking care of myself 360° and I don't expect for people to understand. How I take care of myself, is seeking. The best way in The World I can describe treating other people is showing respect, making sure people get understanding of who I am. I rather deal with people without a problem because I'm a Doctor I rather cure than do anything else. I give people the opportunity they need whether they take it or not. Nobody is going to tell you what to ask so it's up to you.

# Chapter #14
# Choose health over fun

This is important topic because people wouldn't see it clearly. In this chapter I'm not going to tell you, you have to be a health junky or something like that. I'm simply explaining choose health over fun, so we all know our limits, whether we go over them, or not. In this description I'm pointing out pay attention to your health. There are people who depend on substances to get them through or their favorite food, which can be destructive. Choose health over fun put your health before luxury whether it is an activity causing damage to your health or a food causing damage to your health. I'm going to give a few examples: If lifting weights are causing health problems like affecting your heart it's time to switch up the way you work out. That's choosing health over fun because working out would be fun if you got to that point. A example for food would be like in taking food that raises your blood pressure, high cholesterol, creating diabetes, liver failure, kidney problems etc. Choosing health over fun I wouldn't say completely change your diet I would say pay attention to how your diet is affecting you. Once I had high blood pressure and it worried me because I was young. I looked at what I was eating and how it could be; changed it. My high blood pressure was from eating Nutri-Grain bars, a lot of them. So I stopped eating them and it went down back to normal. I didn't stop eating them, I just watched how many I eat and how often. These examples can be used to refer to a bunch of stuff I hope it was helpful.

# Chapter #15
# Why I should use a condom

A conversation like this is major and must be expressed. Why I should use a condom? This plays a major role in Humanity for both Male & Female. If you look at the penis we only think about its two discharges. We look at the penis to discharge sperm and urine. There can also be other discharges, which would take me more studying to figure out. I can say "Even if a condom isn't 100% able to protect you during intercourse" other than the percentage that it can break, this needs to be carefully paid attention to. The spread of infections and diseases are real. I'm pretty sure all people or mostly all people know about these things. Women should protect themselves by making a man use a condom during sex because Males can spread diseases to Females, which is common. I have a sweet side for Females so know a man can get a Female into her emotions just to get her pregnant or not care and spread a disease. A Female has a lot to worry about with dealing with her vagina so a condom should be the first thing on her mind. Her fluids secretions, blood flow from her period cycle so on and so forth should be important to her in the importance of protecting herself. The reason why I should use a condom it's to reduce the spreading of infections & diseases also to reduce catching it from somebody who maybe going through that. You can have safe sex with somebody infected and not catch it; also it's a major risk. These reasons why you should use a condom they are more detailed with safe sex organizations. Get involved with wanting to protect yourself during sex.

# Chapter #16
# I can have more than one Doctor

I presented this book in regards of helping people. I don't want it to be a bias towards other Doctor. I hope even another Doctor can read and appreciate my book. I know I can have more than on Doctor. I have a very nice relationship with my Eye Doctor in Boulder Colorado & me as the patient. We really care to see each other and get into intellectual conversations throughout my visits there. He's the best to me; it's nothing like being around a professional even if they are at work. I appreciate that; I love Medical Doctor's too. I had some of the best relationships with patient Doctor Visits. Even though a Doctor is a Doctor, if they know what they are doing it's great. I can have more *than one Doctor, it's not just about my experiences, it's about looking at it a different way and appreciating your Doctor's.*

# Chapter #17
# Don't let pain go on for too long

This chapter is based on taking care of you, before things get worse. When you find yourself going through pain or something out the ordinary, go see a specialist. Thing's can be treated according to common knowledge of over the counter medication. Then there are other things that need to be treated because there is no other way. The Human body goes through experiences it grows, it gets old, it gets younger, and it dies. When I'm talking about it dies I'm referring to you still being alive and things taking its course. When you cut your finger nails, your hair, or you get a cut, scrap or just skin falling off it dies. Then the body rejuvenates and those things are grown back. I refer to the new growth of skin no matter what stage and age as getting older at least I don't in my Scientific Society. Don't feel pain and just tolerate it without seeking relief through getting treated. It's a duty to take care of you.

# Chapter #18
# Don't judge me outside my robe

People would like to see something that presents what they think of something for reassurance. In this World a lot of things are misunderstood and not given credit over the lack of belonging. I made a clear statement with writing this. Don't judge me outside my robe. The robe I'm speaking about is my Doctor robe. I am a real Doctor not just using the title to make myself have to be in a category of no production. There are many Doctors out there who earn the title and some who just go by the title and can't do the work. I'm a Doctor because I care about curing people establishing my Scientific Practices as a form of Health for people and myself. I shouldn't have to wear a robe to not be judged.

As I am able to write my Doctor Practice, which doesn't divide me from my Scientific Secrets just makes a former standing for me to feel happy & conduct. I plan on going beyond this book and everything known to Mankind. My intentions one day are. To open a Hospital recruiting nurses to help me conduct and establish my Doctor Practice in The World. When I speak about recruiting nurses they are not like the advantage nurse they will be under my Doctor of Medicine Award in 1220 Scientific Society. They will be taught molded and shaped for Top Secret Operations I think its only right I remain the only Doctor, who knows what the future holds. Then we can start the curing process taking it through stages. Don't judge me outside my robe as a Scientist. Don't judge me outside my robe as a Doctor. 1220 Scientific Society operates out of more than 6 dimensions 9 Top Secret Scientific Practices, so your judgments will never be accurate.

# Translation Chinese, German, & Spanish Chapters #1-#18

Chapter #6 couldn't translate into German from English

# 第#1章實現...

　　因為這是一個世界的時代，人們處於失明的階段，在自己內部製造問題：我最好解釋一下我的科學實踐是如何相當於醫學博士學位的。醫學博士是作為醫生所能達到的最高學位。我為什麼要選擇寫"**實現**"？以下是我的主要觀點：

　　如果我們看看《世界》，它就處於停滯狀態。人們被捲入他們的日常活動，並滿足於他們做的事情，即使他們什麼都不做。通過對初學者敞開心扉來實現。進入積極狀態，這一直是令人愉快的，特別是在未來的增長。單單是破壞就是混亂，

沒有大的增長，人們堅持壓迫對方，根本沒有取得進步。實現需要減輕日常負擔，

　　身體和靈魂：幸福更容易達到。一個人必須為自己好，看到結果的變化。實現必須給個人的生活帶來改變。在這裡，我要向這本書的讀者介紹一句話：

　　"改變是人類已知的最可怕的概念"。

　　我從這個剛剛在這個世界上旅行的人那裡學到了這個，
他仍然與人混在一起，
尋找知識。如果你能發現生活中的問題，你可以改變它或離開它。我們都知道我們生活在一個不準備接受別人不同意的其他事情的世界里。這不應該阻止我們作為個人。它應該使我們或個人認識到，並努力實現需要發生

的事情。這就是為什麼我不支持種族主義。我支援女性而不是男性。我只是永遠不會支持他們超過女性。

# Kapitel #1

Da es eine Zeit in der Welt ist, in der Menschen sich in einer Phase der Blindheit befinden, die Probleme in sich selbst schafft; aus sich heraus ist es für mich am besten zu erklären, wie meine wissenschaftlichen Praktiken einem Doktor der Medizin entsprechen. Ein Doktor der Medizin Grad ist der höchste Grad, den man als Arzt erreichen kann. Warum sollte ich mich entscheiden, auf "Come to realization" zu schreiben? Hier ist mein Hauptpunkt:

Wenn wir uns The World anschauen, kommt es zum Stillstand. Die Menschen werden in ihre täglichen Aktivitäten verwickelt und lassen sich für Dinge nieder, die sie tun, auch wenn sie nichts tun. Kommen Sie zur Realisierung, indem Sie aufgeschlossen für Anfänger werden. In den Groove der Positivität, die schon immer angenehm war, vor allem im Wachstum der Zukunft.

Zerstörung allein ist Chaos ein Punkt, an dem es kein größeres Wachstum gibt und die Menschen stecken, sich gegenseitig zu unterdrücken, ohne überhaupt voranzukommen. Die Verwirklichung nimmt den Geist der alltäglichen Last,

Körper und Seele; Glück ist leichter zu erreichen. Eine Person muss gut für sich selbst wollen, um Ergebnisse im Wandel zu sehen. Die Verwirklichung muss Veränderungen im Leben des Einzelnen bringen, die kommen. Genau hier werde ich dem Publikum dieses Buches ein Zitat präsentieren:

"Veränderung ist das gefürchtetste Konzept, das dem Menschen bekannt ist."

Ich habe das von diesem Mann gelernt, der gerade in dieser Welt reist und sich immer noch mit Menschen vermischt, auf der Suche nach Wissen. Wenn Sie sich mit einem Problem in Ihrem Leben identifizieren können, können Sie es ändern oder verlassen. Wir alle wissen, dass wir in einer Welt leben, die nicht bereit ist, andere Dinge zu akzeptieren, mit denen andere Menschen nicht einverstanden sind. Das sollte uns als Individuen nicht aufhalten. Es sollte uns oder den Einzelnen zur Erkenntnis bringen und danach streben, das zu erreichen, was geschehen muss. Deshalb unterstütze ich Rassismus nicht. Ich unterstütze Frauen und nicht Männer. Ich würde sie einfach nie gegenüber Frauen unterstützen.

# Capítulo #1 Ven a la realización......

Ya que es una época en El Mundo, donde la gente está en una etapa de ceguera creando problemas dentro de sí mismas; de sí mismos lo mejor para mí para explicar cómo mis prácticas científicas son equivalentes a un doctorado en medicina. Un Doctor en Medicina es el grado más alto que uno puede alcanzar como médico. ¿Por qué elegiría escribir en "Ven a la realización"? Este es mi punto principal:

Si miramos El Mundo está avanzando en un punto muerto. Las personas están atrapadas en sus actividades diarias y se conforman con cosas que hacen incluso cuando no están haciendo nada. Ven a la realización convirtiéndose en mente abierta para empezar. Entrar en el ritmo de la positividad, que siempre ha sido agradable especialmente en el crecimiento del futuro. La destrucción por sí sola es el caos, un punto en el que no hay un crecimiento importante y la gente se está oprimiendo mutuamente sin salir adelante en absoluto. Llegar a la realización quita la carga cotidiana de la mente, cuerpo, y el alma; la felicidad es más fácil de alcanzar. Una persona debe querer bien para sí misma, para ver los resultados en el cambio. La realización debe traer cambios en la vida del individuo que llega a. Justo aquí voy a presentar una cita a la audiencia de este libro:

"El cambio es el concepto más temido conocido por el hombre".

Aprendí esto de este hombre que viajaba en este mundo todavía mezclándose con la gente, buscando conocimiento. Si puedes identificarte con un problema en tu vida, puedes cambiarlo o dejarlo. Todos sabemos que vivimos en un mundo no listo para aceptar otras cosas con las que otras personas no están de acuerdo. Eso no debería detenernos como individuos. Debe hacer que nosotros o el individuo lleguemos a la realización y se esfuercen por lograr lo que tiene que suceder. Por eso no apoyo el racismo. Apoyo a las hembras y no a los hombres. Nunca los apoyaría sobre las mujeres.

# 第#2章為什麼我不應該放棄。。。

為什麼人們不應該放棄,
不僅僅是失敗和負面的記憶,
而是它使那個人處於懷疑狀態。是的
, 我們可以從我們的試驗和錯誤中學
習。我們可以從錯誤中吸取教訓。為
什麼我不應該放棄提到個人,
這是所有人都應該能夠適應的。

"生活是美好的, 你應該知道你很
重要"。

一個人之所以重要, 有不同的原
因。我們會假設人們給自己自我價值
: 我們知道人們應該自動愛自己另一
個原因是, 世界是如何走向的, 不是

每個人，但有些人誰添加的東西到世界，說明其他人在一個巨大的水平，他們比重要。我們可以舉出一些對人類有用的東西：廁所的發明

**紙，通過發明鞋子保護一隻**腳。即使人們不想接受它，

他們也很重要。另一個原因，為什麼人們應該知道他們很重要，因為當你不愛自己，別人在那裡愛：關心你你通過給世界添加一些東西很重要，因為你愛你自己，

或者只是別人愛你。這是一個簡短的為什麼你或我不應該放棄。

# Kapitel #2 Warum ich nicht aufgeben sollte....

Warum Menschen nicht aufgeben sollten, ist nicht nur Scheitern und ein negatives Gedächtnis, aber es hält diese Person in einem Zustand des Zweifels. Ja, wir können aus unseren Prüfungen und Fehlern lernen. Wir können aus unseren Fehlern lernen. Warum ich nicht aufgeben sollte, mich auf den Einzelnen zu beziehen, auf etwas, auf das sich alle Menschen einstellen können sollten.

"Das Leben ist schön und du solltest wissen, dass du wichtig bist."

Es gibt verschiedene Gründe, warum eine Person wichtig wäre. Wir würden davon ausgehen, dass die Menschen sich selbst wert geben; wir wissen, dass die Menschen sich automatisch selbst lieben sollten. Ein weiterer Grund ist, wie die Welt geht, nicht jeder, aber es gibt Menschen, die der Welt Dinge hinzufügen, die anderen Menschen auf einer massiven Ebene helfen, die mehr als wichtig sind. Wir können ein paar Dinge nennen, die für die Menschheit nützlich waren: Die Erfindung der Toilette

Papier, die eigenen Füße durch die Erfindung von Schuhen schützen. Die Menschen sind wichtig, auch wenn sie es nicht akzeptieren wollen. Ein weiterer Grund, warum Menschen wissen sollten, dass sie wichtig sind, denn wenn du dich selbst nicht liebst, liebt jemand anderes da draußen; sich um Sie kümmert. Du bist wichtig, indem du der Welt etwas hinzufügst, weil du dich selbst oder einfach jemand anderen liebst, der dich liebt. Das ist eine kurze Frage, warum Sie oder ich nicht aufgeben sollten.

# Capítulo #2 Por qué no debería rendirme...

Por qué la gente no debe rendirse, no sólo es un fracaso y una memoria negativa, sino que mantiene a esa persona en un estado de duda. Sí, podemos aprender de nuestras pruebas y errores. Podemos aprender de nuestros errores. ¿Por qué no debería dejar de referirme al individuo, algo a lo que todas las personas deberían ser capaces de adaptarse?

"La vida es hermosa y debes saber que importas".

Hay diferentes razones por las que una persona importaría. Asumiríamos que la gente se da autoestima; sabemos que la gente debe amarse automáticamente a sí misma. Otra razón es cómo va El Mundo, no todo el mundo, pero hay gente que añade cosas a El

Mundo, que ayudan a otras personas a un nivel masivo que más que importa. Podemos nombrar algunas cosas que fueron útiles para la Humanidad: La invención del inodoro papel, protegiendo los pies inventando zapatos. La gente sí importa aunque no quiera aceptarlo. Otra razón por la que la gente debe saber que importa, porque cuando no te amas a ti mismo alguien más ama; se preocupa por ti. Importas añadiendo algo a El Mundo, porque te amas a ti mismo o simplemente a alguien más amándote. Es un resumen de por qué tú o yo no deberíamos rendirme.

# 第#3章
# 什麼是健康？

　　健康的事情，我們可以用運動作為第一，得到適當的休息是第二個。然後你有你管理你的身體的方式和你如何與人互動。如果我們把健康看在應有的水準上，如果我們健康，我們會說明另一個人保持健康或保持健康。傳播良好的氛圍是健康的。不為清理別人的爛攤子而驕傲是健康的。我之所以說這些話，是為了幫助人們打開他們思想的新部分，使他們的能力不受錯誤判斷、抵制或只是不關心健康所阻礙。當一個人能夠思考和知道什麼是正確的，有它應用在他們的生活中是一個偉大的健康。人腦裡有

很多垃圾，它每天在幾秒鐘內傳播，一夜之間傳播。健康的一種形式是擺脫那些東西變得更加投入

你自己，並成為使地球健康的一部分。

# Kapitel #3 Was ist gesund?

Dinge, die gesund sind, können wir Übung als die erste verwenden, immer richtige Ruhe ist die zweite. Dann haben Sie die Art und Weise, wie Sie Ihren Körper verwalten und wie Sie mit Menschen interagieren. Wenn wir die Gesundheit auf dem Niveau betrachten, das wir sollten, wenn wir gesund sind, würden wir einer anderen Person helfen, gesund zu werden oder ihre Gesundheit zu erhalten. Gute Stimmung zu verbreiten ist gesund. Nicht stolz darauf zu sein, das Chaos eines anderen zu säubern, ist gesund. Der Grund, warum ich sage, dass diese Dinge darin besteht, den Menschen zu helfen, einen neuen Teil ihres Geistes zu öffnen und ihre Fähigkeiten nicht durch falsches Urteilsvermögen, Widerstand oder einfach nicht darum zu kümmern, gesund zu sein, zu behindern. Wenn eine Person denken und wissen kann, was richtig ist, ist es eine große Gesundheit, wenn sie in ihrem Leben angewendet wird. Es gibt eine Menge Müll in den Gehirnen der Menschen und es breitet sich täglich, über Nacht in der Angelegenheit von Sekunden. Eine Form der Gesundheit wäre, dieses Zeug loszuwerden, mehr in sich selbst zu werden und ein Teil der Herstellung von The Planet Healthy zu sein.

# Capítulo #3 ¿Qué es saludable?

Cosas que son saludables, podemos usar el ejercicio siendo el primero, descansando adecuadamente siendo el segundo. Entonces tienes la forma en que manejas tu cuerpo y cómo interactúas con la gente. Si miramos la salud en el nivel que deberíamos, si estamos sanos ayudaríamos a otra persona a recuperarse o mantener su salud. Difundir buenas vibraciones es saludable. No ser orgulloso de limpiar el desorden de otra persona es saludable. La razón por la que digo estas cosas es para ayudar a las personas a abrir una nueva parte de sus mentes, y hacer que sus capacidades no se vean obstaculizadas por el falso juicio, la resistencia o simplemente no preocuparse por estar sanos. Cuando una persona puede pensar y saber lo que es correcto, tenerlo aplicado en sus vidas es una gran salud. Hay mucha basura en el cerebro de la gente y se propaga diariamente, de la noche a la mañana en cuestión de segundos. Una forma de salud sería deshacerse de que las cosas se convierten más en ti mismo y ser parte de hacer El Planeta Saludable.

# 第#4章
# 如何擺脫自殺的念實

　　自殺是我想討論的一個主要話題。這是我感到高興的事情，表達了我的擔憂。我想知道，我有兩個或兩個以上的事件，我說明一個人，意識到，自殺不適合他們。很久以前，大概在2009年，我和一個面臨25歲生活的人在一起。我不記得他的指控，但他害怕坐牢。他無數次告訴我，當他到監獄時，他要上吊自殺。他想上吊自殺的理由是他不知道監獄是什麼樣子的。幾個星期，他會說「他要自殺，他要自殺」，不斷結束：在每天。我會

跟他說好話，讓他知道，甚至
雖然他會在監獄裡，他的母親需要他
。一開始，他不會接受他需要活下去
。然後有一天，他面帶微笑地告訴我"
他不會自殺的"。當他對我說，他只是
說，走開了。之後他什麼也沒說我覺
得有成就感，然後我知道他自由了。
他擺脫了被過度帶走的念頭：他需要
結束它。這是不必要的壓力去通過。
同一天過了一會兒，我和他聊了聊：
他會和我分享，他的母親要送他包裹
：錢，所以他很高興。這是我說明某
人自殺的最大經驗。我不應該說
「這是我最大的經歷」，
因為每當某人自殺時，
它都是巨大的。我說明預防自殺的下
一次經歷是在科羅拉多。在科羅拉多
的博爾德，一個無家可歸的人在垃圾
箱後面，在嚴寒中，他是一個老人：
他說："他想死在那裡，沒有人c.。。

他"。他同意他很冷，想取暖。他凍僵了，為了保暖，會自己小便。我叫了救護車，他們來了，把他帶走了。我感覺很好，我又救了一條命。我記得第一次。我認為那些沒有機會拯救那樣生命的人不知道會有什麼感覺。太神奇了，我甚至試圖更進一步，把它作為一個職業。然後，我被打在臉上，因為它說："你需要一個碩士學位是一個自殺預防顧問"。我知道我根本不需要學位，因為我幫助人們，從想通過它。阻止自殺的方法，你自己，就是看人生，不放棄。管好事情，與人交談，知道你並不孤單。不要羞辱自己：在最壞的情況下試著睡一覺。我希望我是一個真正的，自殺預防顧問，在那裡我可以在24小時的電話，只是為了顯示另一種方式，而不是把你的...

# Kapitel #4 Hoo, um aus dem Wunsch, Selbstmord zu begehen

Selbstmord ist ein großes Thema, das ich ansprechen kann. Darüber freue ich mich, dass ich meine Bedenken zum Ausdruck bringe. Ich möchte, dass es bekannt ist, ich habe zwei oder mehr Vorfälle, bei denen ich einer Person geholfen habe, zu der Erkenntnis zu kommen, welcher Selbstmord nichts für sie war. Vor langer Zeit wahrscheinlich im Jahr 2009 war ich um einen Kerl, der 25 Jahre zum Leben konfrontiert. Ich erinnere mich nicht an seine Anschuldigungen, aber er hatte Angst vor dem Gefängnis. Er erzählte mir unzählige Male, als er ins Gefängnis kam, würde er sich erhängen. Seine Gründe, sich erhängen zu wollen, war, dass er nicht wusste, wie Gefängnis war. Wochenlang sagte er: "Er wollte sich umbringen, er wollte sich umbringen", ständig vorbei; über jeden Tag. Ich würde gutes mit ihm sprechen und ihn wissen lassen, obwohl er im Gefängnis saß, brauchte ihn seine Mutter. Am Anfang würde er nicht akzeptieren, dass er leben muss. Eines Tages sagte er mir mit einem breiten Lächeln im Gesicht: "Er wollte sich nicht umbringen". Als er es mir sagte, sagte er es einfach und ging weg. Danach sagte er nichts mehr. Ich fühlte mich vollendet, dann wusste ich, dass er frei war. Er war frei von seinem Verstand, der übernommen wurde; indem er es beenden muss. Das ist unnötiger Druck, durchzugehen. Nach einer Weile am selben Tag redeten ich und er; er würde mit mir teilen, seine Mutter wird ihm Pakete schicken; Geld, also freute er sich darüber. Das war meine größte Erfahrung, jemandem beim Selbstmord zu helfen. Ich sollte nicht sagen: "Das ist meine größte Erfahrung", denn jedes Mal, wenn man jemanden davon abhält, Selbstmord zu begehen, ist es groß. Meine nächste Erfahrung in der Unterstützung der Suizidprävention war in Colorado. In Boulder Colorado war ein Obdachloser hinter einem Mülleimer, in der eisigen Kälte war er ein alter Mann; er sagte: "Er will dort sterben, niemand c ... ihn". Er stimmte zu, dass er kalt war, und wollte warm sein. Er war eiskalt und urinierte auf sich selbst, nur um warm zu bleiben. Ich rief den Krankenwagen und sie kamen und nahmen ihn weg. Ich fühlte mich so gut, dass ich ein anderes Leben rettete. Ich erinnerte mich an das erste Mal. Ich glaube nicht, dass Menschen, die keine Chance hatten, ein Leben wie dieses zu retten, wussten, wie es sich anfühlen würde. Es ist erstaunlich, ich habe sogar versucht, es einen Schritt weiter zu gehen und es als Karriere zu tun. Dann wurde mir ins Gesicht geschlagen, weil es heißt: "Du brauchst einen Master-Abschluss, um ein Suicide Prevention Counselor zu sein". Ich wusste, dass ich überhaupt keinen Abschluss brauchte, weil ich Menschen geholfen habe, aus dem Wunsch herauszukommen, damit durchzukommen. Der Weg, sich selbst davon abzuhalten, Selbstmord zu begehen, besteht darin, das Leben zu betrachten, nicht aufzugeben. Denken Sie über materie, sprechen Sie mit Menschen, wissen Sie, dass Sie nicht allein in der Welt sind. Beschämen Sie sich nicht; versuchen, es im schlimmsten Fall auszuschlafen. Ich wünschte, ich wäre ein tatsächlicher, Suicide Prevention Counselor, wo ich auf 24 Stunden Anruf sein kann, nur um einen anderen Weg zu zeigen, anstatt Ihre ...

# Capítulo #4 Cómo salir de querer suicidarse

El suicidio es un tema importante para mí. Es algo por lo que me siento feliz, expresando mis preocupaciones. Quiero que se sepa, tengo dos o más incidentes en los que ayudé a una persona, a llegar a la comprensión, que el suicidio no era para ellos. A lo largo del tiempo, probablemente en el año 2009, yo estaba cerca de un tipo que se enfrentaba a 25 años de vida. No recuerdo sus cargos, pero tenía miedo de la cárcel. Me dijo incontables veces que cuando llegara a prisión se iba a ahorcar. Sus razones para querer ahorcarse era que no sabía cómo era la cárcel. Durante semanas decía "Se iba a suicidar, se iba a suicidar", constantemente más; a diario. Yo le decía cosas buenas y le hacía saber, incluso aunque estaría en la cárcel, su madre lo necesitaba. Al principio, no aceptaría que necesita vivir. Luego, un día, con una gran sonrisa en la cara, me dijo: "No se iba a suicidar". Cuando me lo dijo, lo dijo y se fue. Ni siquiera dijo nada después. Me sentí logrado entonces supe que era libre. Estaba libre de que su mente fuera tomada en exceso; por él necesita terminarlo. Esa es una presión innecesaria para pasar. Después de un tiempo en el mismo día, yo y él hablamos; él compartiría conmigo, su madre va a enviarle paquetes; dinero, así que estaba feliz por eso. Esta fue mi mayor experiencia en ayudar a alguien a salir de suicidarse. No debería decir "Esta es mi mayor experiencia", porque cada vez que evitas que alguien se suicide, es grande. Mi siguiente experiencia en ayudar a la prevención del suicidio fue en Colorado. En Boulder Colorado, un vagabundo estaba detrás de un contenedor de basura, en el frío helado, era un anciano; él dijo: "Él quiere morir detrás de allí, nadie c ... él". Aceptó que tenía frío y quería estar caliente. Estaba helado y orinaba sobre sí mismo, sólo para mantenerse caliente. Llamé a la ambulancia y vinieron y se lo llevaron. Me sentí tan bien que salvé otra vida. Me acordé la primera vez. No creo que la gente, que no ha tenido la oportunidad de salvar una vida así, supiera cómo se sentiría. Es increíble, incluso traté de dar un paso más allá y hacerlo como una carrera. Luego me dieron una bofetada en la cara, porque dice "Necesitas un Máster para ser consejero de prevención del suicidio". Sabía que no necesitaba un título en absoluto, porque ayudé a la gente, a salir de querer seguir adelante con eso. La manera de evitar, a ti mismo, suicidarse es mirar la vida, no rendirse. La mente sobre la materia, hablar con la gente, saber que no estás solo en El Mundo. No te avergüences; tratar de dormir en el peor de los casos. Me gustaría ser un verdadero, consejero de prevención del suicidio, donde puedo estar en llamada las 24 horas, sólo para mostrar otra manera, en lugar de tomar su ...

# 第#5章
# 為什麼衛生很重要
# ？

　　作為一名醫生，試圖讓我的理解通過的人，我可能不得不說的東西，人們已經知道，同時我使用科學實踐。衛生之所以重要，是因為衛生條件差會給人體帶來重大問題。在仔細研究中，防止對疫情最常見的反應的方法是清潔。衛生對於減少身體在不被照顧時可能散發出的惡臭氣味很重要。如果人們不注意衛生，就會導致世界人口的一定比例受到影響，而其他百分比的人會受到影響。大多數人可以在泥土中玩耍，只要他們正確清

潔自己，就不會有負面反應。不要太
參與讓秘密從我的

科學社會，人們需要找出每一種方法
，將清洗他們，而不是造成負面反應
，在解決方案或護理產品的化學品。
人們處於進化狀態，這意味著要彌補
衛生方面的不足：確保它是一個優先
事項，而不是一個選項。

# Kapitel #5 Warum Hygiene wichtig ist?

Als Doktor, der versucht, mein Verständnis zu den Menschen zu vermitteln, muss ich vielleicht Dinge sagen, die die Leute bereits kennen, und gleichzeitig benerste ich wissenschaftliche Praktiken. Der Grund, warum Hygiene wichtig ist, ist, weil schlechte Hygiene große Probleme für den menschlichen Körper verursachen kann. Unter genauer Studie ist der Weg, um die häufigsten Reaktionen auf Ausbrüche zu verhindern, Sauberkeit. Hygiene ist wichtig, um den üblen Geruch zu reduzieren, den der Körper auslassen könnte, wenn er nicht gepflegt wird. Wenn die Menschen nicht auf Hygiene achten würden, würde dies dazu führen, dass ein Prozentsatz der Weltbevölkerung betroffen ist, die anderen Prozentsätze der Menschen, die dies tun. Die meisten Menschen können im

Dreck spielen und haben keine negative Reaktion, solange sie sich richtig reinigen. Um sich nicht zu sehr damit zu beschäftigen, The Secrets aus meiner Wissenschaftlichen Gesellschaft herauszulassen, müssen die Menschen jede Methode herausfinden, die sie reinigt und keine negative Reaktion auf die Chemikalien in den Lösungen oder Pflegeprodukten hervorruft. Die Menschen sind in The State of Evolution, was bedeutet, dass sie ...

# Capítulo #5 ¿Por qué es importante la higiene?

Como Doctor, tratando de llevar mi comprensión a la gente, tal vez tenga que decir cosas que la gente ya sabe, y al mismo tiempo estoy usando prácticas científicas. La razón por la que la higiene es importante es porque una mala higiene puede causar problemas importantes.al cuerpo humano. Bajo un estudio cercano, la forma de prevenir las reacciones más comunes a los brotes es la limpieza. La higiene es importante para reducir el olor fétido que el cuerpo podría dejar salir, cuando no se cuida. Si la gente no prestara atención a la higiene, causaría que un porcentaje de la población mundial afectara, los otros porcentajes de personas que lo hacen. La mayoría de las personas pueden jugar en la suciedad y no tener una reacción negativa siempre y cuando se limpien correctamente. Para no involucrarse demasiado en dejar salir a Los Secretos de mi Sociedad Científica, la gente necesita averiguar todos los métodos que los limpiarán y no causar una reacción negativa, a los productos químicos en las soluciones o productos de cuidado. La gente está en El Estado de la Evolución, lo que significa recoger t ...

# 第#6章我最後一次遇到心理健康和我幫助的科學理由

我最後一次與心理健康的接觸是殘酷的，但讓我先說：

當我7歲滿8歲的時候，我從奧爾巴尼N.Y的一個兩層樓的窗戶上摔了下來，這個窗戶位於1994年的三一街。我過去常嚇唬我媽媽，告訴她我要自殺，所以我被投入了心理健康。隨著年齡的增長，我處理心理健康與顧問和專家談論的問題。所以基本上我一直在處理他們斷斷續續，直到2021年。我

試圖接受評估，
以證明我年輕時所說的一切是假的，
他們不讓我這麼做。出於一些奇怪的
原因，
你永遠無法抹去心理健康記錄。我已
經嘗試過多次這樣做，
這虛假的指控阻礙我在很多領域，
特別是心理健康文件線索。我可以把
我的記錄密封和刪除，
但我不能抹去我的心理健康記錄，
這很奇怪。我最後一次見到他們是虐
待他們。我在雪地里住了幾個小時，
我決定去醫院檢查背部疼痛：可能的
霜凍叮咬。我過夜，確保我的...
足以填寫表格，說："這不是對自己或
其他人的威脅，我有我的耳環：戒指
在我的手指上」。所以他們沒有為此
煩惱。我測試了冠狀病毒的陰性，所
以我最終被轉移到非冠狀病毒單位。
我在那裡做正常的事情，

我不得不通知社會保障,
以及聯邦法院北區奧爾巴尼, 紐約州
- 我的權利被侵犯,
所以他們知道。我正在和一位醫生見
面, 醫生只會說「我需要藥物」,
因為我對他跟我說話或試圖讓我留在
醫院感到憤怒。我變得非常挑釁非常
不聽話。我用拳頭打碎了窗戶,
把東西扔遍了。這不是因為我的精神
狀態,
這是因為他們試圖搞砸我的生活,
與假診斷,
並沒有做一個適當的評估。我甚至告
訴我的出版公司作者之家, "更新我的
帳戶名人作者"。我問"他們查我的書"
。我告訴他們"我從來沒做過任何事...
科學家;我不能透露維度或我的理
論或實踐方法。要麼你明白,
我知道我在說什麼,

要麼就像一個死胡同,
因為那時我忍不住。

# Capítulo #6 Mi último encuentro con salud mental y mis razones científicas para ayudar

Mi último encuentro con Salud Mental fue brutal, pero permítanme comenzar diciendo:

Cuando tenía 7 años cumpliendo 8 años, me caí por una ventana de dos pisos en Albany N.Y, en Trinity St 1994. Solía asustar a mi madre diciéndole que me iba a suicidar, así que me me pusieron en Salud Mental. A medida que crecía, me ocupé de salud mental hablando con consejeros y especialistas sobre temas. Así que básicamente he estado lidiando con ellos de vez en cuando hasta 2021. Traté de ir bajo evaluaciones para probar que lo que decía cuando era joven era falso, no me dejaban hacer eso. Por alguna extraña razón nunca se puede borrar un registro de salud mental. He intentado hacer esto varias veces, lo que falsas acusaciones me obstaculizan en muchas áreas, especialmente ese rastro de papel de salud mental. Podría sellar mi disco y borrarlo, pero no puedo borrar mi historial de Salud Mental, eso es extraño. Mi último encuentro con ellos fue abuso de su parte para mí. Estuve en la nieve durante horas decidí ir al Hospital y que me revisaran por dolor de espalda; posible picadura de escarcha. Me alojé toda la noche, me aseguré de que mi ...

lo suficientemente agradable como para llenar un formulario, diciendo : "No fue una amenaza para mí u otras personas, yo teniendo mis pendientes; anillos en mis dedos". Así que no me molestaron por eso. Probé negativo para El Coronavirus, así que finalmente me trasladaron a la Unidad de No Coronavirus. Yo estaba allí haciendo cosas normales, tuve que notificar al Seguro Social, así como al Tribunal Federal del Distrito Norte albany, N.Y- que mis derechos estaban siendo violados, por lo que estaban al tanto. Me reunía con un doctor que me decía "necesito medicación" porque me enojo porque me enojé con él hablando conmigo o tratando de hacerme quedarme en el Hospital. Me volví muy desafiante muy desobediente. Rompí ventanas con puñetazos tirados cosas por todas partes. Esto no fue por mi Estado Mental, esto fue porque trataron de arruinar mi vida, con un diagnóstico falso y no hacer una evaluación adecuada. Incluso le dije a mi Editorial Author House: "Para actualizar mi cuenta a Celebrity Author". Les pedí que buscaran mis libros". Les dije "Nunca hice nada...

# 第 7 章強姦犯需要説明

　　所以醫生我不能抨擊那些我覺得違背所有生活道德的人。強姦犯的道德，是一團糟。強姦犯對女性的傷害比世界上任何事情都大。"強姦犯需要説明"需要在全球生效。沒有必要強姦女性：因為我是一個科學家，我做了很多工作和研究強姦犯。我知道他們的動機和為什麼他們強姦。我不明白他們為什麼選擇這樣做，但我明白。強姦犯不管你怎麼看都需要説明她們因對女性犯下的罪行而需要受到治療和懲罰。原因，為什麼，我説"女性"，因為它發生在女性，所有年齡段，在我的研究中，一個男人會陰謀反對女性的性快感，因為他覺得佔主導地位&歸類為女性的弱點。他們利用自己的力量或通過操縱來引誘別有用心的女性。強姦犯可以強姦作為後果的標誌，感覺他們做錯了。強姦犯需要說明，因為他們不去想...

# Kapitel 7
# Vergewaltiger braucht Hilfe

Ein Doktor, den ich nicht bash enther die Menschen, die ich fühle, gegen jede Ethik des Lebens gehen. Die Moral eines Vergewaltigers ist durcheinander. Vergewaltiger haben einem Weibchen mehr Unrecht getan als alles andere in der Welt. "Rapist braucht Hilfe" muss global in Kraft treten. Es besteht keine Notwendigkeit, eine Frau zu vergewaltigen; weil ich Wissenschaftler bin, habe ich viel Arbeit gemacht und über Vergewaltiger studiert. Ich kenne ihre Motive und warum sie vergewaltigen. Ich verstehe nicht, warum sie sich dafür entscheiden würden, aber ich verstehe. Ein Vergewaltiger, egal wie man ihn betrachtet, braucht Hilfe. Sie müssen für ihre

Verbrechen gegen Frauen behandelt und bestraft werden. Der Grund, warum, ich sage "Frauen", weil es Frauen passiert, aller Altersgruppen, in meinem Studium würde ein Mann gegen eine Frau für sexuelle Freuden planen, weil er fühlt sich dominiert & klassifiziert ein Weibchen als Schwäche. Sie nutzen ihre Stärke oder locken ein Weibchen mit Hintergedanken, durch Manipulation. Ein Vergewaltiger kann als Zeichen der Konsequenz vergewaltigen und das Gefühl haben, falsch gemacht worden zu sein. Ein Vergewaltiger braucht Hilfe, weil er nicht an die Tr ...

# Capítulo #7 Violador necesita ayuda

Así que un Doctor no puedo golpear a la gente que siento que va en contra de toda ética de vivir. La moral de un violador.está arruinada. Los violadores le han hecho más mal a una mujer que cualquier otra cosa en el mundo. "El violador necesita ayuda" necesita entrar en vigor a nivel mundial. No hay necesidad de violar a una mujer; porque soy científico he hecho mucho trabajo y estudio sobre violador. Conozco sus motivos y por qué violan. No entiendo por qué elegirían hacerlo, pero lo entiendo. Un violador no importa cómo lo mires necesita ayuda. Necesitan ser tratados y o castigados por sus crímenes contra las mujeres. La razón, por qué, digo "Hembras" porque le pasa a las hembras, de todas las edades, en mis estudios un hombre conspiraría contra una mujer por placeres sexuales, porque se siente dominante & clasifica a una mujer como debilidad. Usan su fuerza o atrayendo a una hembra con motivos ocultos, a través de la manipulación. Un violador puede violar como una señal de consecuencia, sintiendo que se hicieron mal. Un violador necesita ayuda porque no piensa en el tr ...

# 第#8章冥想能説明我嗎？

　　人們已經知道音樂是一種醫學形式。它通常觸動靈魂，娛樂人們。它現在在《世界》里很大，所以人們可以享受它。這一章不是關於音樂，它是關於冥想。冥想能説明我嗎？讓我從我的角度來看冥想，以及它如何幫助別人。十多年來，我一直在做冥想秘密冥想，將意識轉化為中心。冥想可以重置偏離軌道的頭腦。我沒有說這是第一次冥想後會發生的事情。我從未放棄冥想，所以我看到的不僅僅是冥想的結果。當你審視自己時，很難理解你需要更加謙遜，或者你需要後退一步，尤其

是在炎熱的時刻。當你期待冥想來說明你度過一天，你改變你的概念和不同的能量，你正在處理。我和別人一起進行的冥想，
它以我為指導。我引導人們通過堅實的米...

# Kapitel #8 Kann Meditation mir helfen?

Die Leute wissen bereits, dass Musik eine Form der Medizin ist. Es berührt in der Regel die Seele und unterhält die Menschen. Es ist groß in der Welt im Moment, so dass die Menschen es genießen können. In diesem Kapitel geht es nicht um Musik, es geht um Meditation. Kann mir Meditation helfen? Lassen Sie mich über Meditation aus meiner Sicht sprechen und wie sie jemandem helfen kann. Ich mache seit über einem Jahrzehnt Meditationen, die das Bewusstsein in Zentrum verwandeln. Meditation kann einen Geist zurücksetzen, der aus der Spur ist. Ich habe nicht gesagt, dass es etwas war, das nach der ersten Meditation passieren wird. Ich habe nie aufgegeben zu meditieren, also habe ich mehr als die Ergebnisse davon gesehen. Wenn sie sich selbst betrachten, ist es schwer zu verstehen, dass man demütiger sein muss oder einen Schritt zurück machen muss, besonders in der Hitze des Augenblicks. Wenn du auf Meditation schaust, um dir durch den Tag zu helfen, änderst du dein Konzept und deine andere Energie, mit der du es zu tun hast. Die Meditationen, die ich mit anderen Menschen führe, werden von mir geleitet. Ich führe die Menschen durch solide m ...

# Capítulo #8 ¿Puede ayudarme la meditación?

La gente ya sabe que la música es una forma de medicina. Por lo general toca el alma y entretiene a la gente. Es grande en El Mundo en este momento, para que la gente pueda disfrutarlo. Este capítulo no trata sobre la música se trata de meditación. ¿Puede ayudarme la meditación? Permítanme hablar de meditación desde mi punto de vista y cómo puede ayudar a alguien. He estado haciendo meditaciones durante más de una década meditaciones secretas que transforman la conciencia en el centro. La meditación puede restablecer una mente que está fuera de lugar. No dije que fuera algo que sucederá después de la primera meditación. Nunca renuncié a meditar, así que he visto más que los resultados de hacerlo. Cuando te miras a ti mismo, es difícil entender que necesitas ser más humilde o que necesitas dar un paso atrás, especialmente en el calor del momento. Cuando miras hacia la meditación para ayudarte a través del día, cambias tu concepto y tu diferente energía con la que estás lidiando. Las meditaciones que llevo a cabo con otras personas son guiadas por mí. Guio a la gente a través de m sólido ...

# 第#9章
# 看待憤怒的另一種方式

　　當我開始打破這個，我知道人們可能會認為"我聽到這一切之前"。我會說「真的」，
憤怒這是另一種看待它的方式。憤怒破壞了它破壞所有美好氛圍的樂趣，可以壓倒所有其他情緒。我相信所有的情緒都應該被認可，並由個人控制。憤怒來來去去，
即使是世界上最憤怒的人也喜歡放鬆，
如果他們能的話。如果我們能從科學的角度把憤怒分解，那就是一種平衡

。這是一種被歸類為一種情感的機制，它提醒一個人更深層次的分歧。這是一種對所發生的事情的拒絕。它從來沒有被記錄或告訴一個人無緣無故生氣。就像我說的"處理憤怒的最佳方式"就是不要對憤怒採取行動。讓它來來去去，

因為沒有人能說我永遠不會生氣。當我生氣的時候，他們可以指望，

我該怎麼處理它。如果你注意這一章中所說的話，你可以清楚地看到，另一種方式來尋找一個。。。

# Kapitel #9 Eine andere Möglichkeit, Wut zu sehen

Als ich anfange, dies aufzubrechen, weiß ich, dass die Leute wahrscheinlich denken werden: "Ich habe das alles schon einmal gehört". Ich würde sagen "Wirklich", Wut ist dies eine andere Art, es zu betrachten. Wut verdirbt den Spaß, er verdirbt alle guten Stimmungen und kann alle anderen Emotionen überwältigen. Ich glaube, dass alle Emotionen erkannt werden sollten und unter der Kontrolle des Individuums. Wut kommt und geht sogar die wütendste Person in The World liebt es, entspannt zu sein, wenn sie können. Wenn wir den Ärger aus wissenschaftlicher Sicht abbauen können, dann ist das ein Gleichgewicht. Es ist ein Mechanismus, der als Emotion klassifiziert wird, der eine Person vor einer tieferen Meinungsverschiedenheit warnt. Es ist eine Form der Ablehnung von etwas, das aufgetreten ist. Es wurde nie dokumentiert oder gesagt, dass eine Person ohne Grund wütend war. Wie ich sagte "Der beste Weg, um mit Wut umzugehen" ist nicht darauf zu handeln. Lass es kommen und gehen, weil niemand sagen kann, dass ich nie wütend werde. Sie können sich darauf verlassen, wenn ich wütend werde, wie ich damit umgehen werde. Wenn Sie darauf achten, was in diesem Kapitel gesagt wurde, können Sie deutlich sehen, eine andere Möglichkeit, eine ...

# Capítulo #9 Otra forma de ver la ira

A medida que empiezo a desglose esto sé que la gente probablemente pensará "lo escuché todo antes". Yo diría "Realmente", la ira esta es otra manera de verlo. La ira estropea la diversión que estropea todas las buenas vibraciones y puede dominar todas las demás emociones. Creo que todas las emociones deben ser reconocidas y bajo el control del individuo. La ira va y viene incluso la persona más enfadada del mundo le encanta estar relajado si puede. Si podemos romper la ira desde el punto de vista científico es un equilibrio. Es un mecanismo clasificado como una emoción que alerta a una persona de un desacuerdo más profundo. Es una forma de rechazo a algo que ocurrió. Nunca se documentó ni se le dijo que una persona estaba enojada sin razón. Como dije "La mejor manera de lidiar con la ira" es no actuar en ello. Déjalo ir y venir porque nadie puede decir que nunca me voy a enojar. Pueden contar con cuando me enoje, cómo voy a manejarlo. Si prestas atención a lo que se dijo en este capítulo puedes ver claramente, otra forma de...

# 第#10章我不是醫生我是科學博士

我寫這本書的理由是證明我有沒有醫學院所需要的東西。我的科學實踐相當於醫學博士學位。我不是醫生我是人類進化的科學博士事實上，我解決人類的人類存在多重問題。自從我以科學家的身份認真對待我的研究以來，我情不自禁地一路走來。我是一名絕密科學家，我專攻許多不同的科學領域。如果我這樣研究的話，我可能會成為終極醫生之一。讓我來瞭解一下，

我很欣賞在醫院工作的好醫生，

從手術到檢查，

履行醫療職責。我必須把什麼帶到桌

子上是超越這一點。世界上的每個人都不聽好消息，什麼會幫助他們，等等。這並不意味著他們不知道。我要說，大多數問題都可以解決，地球可以朝著更有利於人類的不同方向前進。我拿我的科學公關...

說明世界上對人類無害的行動。1220科學協會我是指揮官和酋長，

所有的做法都很敏感，

所以僅自己在外面看。我達到了一個水準，使我在所有科學社會社區與70億人在世界只有70萬人的潛力。確切地說，他們可能是死是活。特別是作為一個科學家，

世界上大多數人心胸狹窄，

他們甚至不想學習，然後繼續，

他們寧願放棄機會。不僅僅是說1220科學學會有80年的時間從2020年統治到2100年。這是一個祝福，我想讓很多很好的研究和文檔發生在那個時候

。我有幾個人在等待名單上只是為了知道 1220 是什麼意思， 事實證明，他們沒有作出削減。所以我沒有失去任何東西， 我知道 1220 仍然受到保護。

# Kapitel #10 Ich bin kein Arzt, ich bin ein wissenschaftlicher Arzt

Mein Grund, dieses Buch zu schreiben, ist zu beweisen, dass ich das Zeug dazu habe, ohne medizinische Schule. Meine wissenschaftlichen Praxen sind gleichbedeutend mit einem Doktor der Medizin Grad. Ich bin kein Doktor, ich bin ein wissenschaftlicher Doktor der menschlichen Evolution. Es gibt mehrere Probleme mit der Menschheit, die ich an menschenanspreche, um tatsächlich zu sein. Da ich mein Studium als Wissenschaftler ernst nahm, konnte ich nicht anders, um den ganzen Weg zu gehen. Ich bin ein Top Secret Scientist Ich spezialisiere mich auf viele verschiedene Bereiche der

Wissenschaft. Ich wäre wahrscheinlich einer der ultimativen Ärzte, wenn ich diese Art zu gehen studieren. Lassen Sie mich wissen, dass ich gute Ärzte schätze, die im Krankenhaus arbeiten und medizinische Aufgaben von Operationen bis hin zu Kontrolluntersuchungen erfüllen. Was ich an den Tisch bringen muss, ist darüber hinaus. Jeder in der Welt hört nicht auf gute Nachrichten, was ihnen helfen wird, etc. Das bedeutet nicht, dass sie sich dessen nicht bewusst sind. Ich werde sagen, dass die meisten Probleme gelöst werden können und der Planet auf seinem Kurs in eine andere Richtung sein kann, die für die Menschheit vorteilhafter ist. Ich nehme meine wissenschaftliche Pr ... Operationen, um in der Welt zu helfen, die für den Menschen nicht schädlich sind. 1220 Wissenschaftliche Gesellschaft Ich bin Kommandant und Chief alle Praktiken sind empfindlich, so ist es nur ich auf der Außenseite Blick nach innen. Ich habe ein Niveau erreicht, das mich zu einer Million in allen Gemeinschaften der

Wissenschaftlichen Gesellschaft mit 7 Milliarden Menschen in der Welt gemacht hat, nur 700.000 Menschen haben das Potenzial. Sie könnten tot oder lebendig sein, um genau zu sein. Zumal eine Wissenschaftlermehrheit der Menschen in der Welt verschlossen ist, sie wollen nicht einmal lernen, dann weitermachen, verstreichen sie eher die Chance. Nicht nur zu sagen, 1220 Wissenschaftliche Gesellschaft hat 80 Jahre, um von 2020 bis 2100 zu regieren. Das ist ein Segen, den ich in dieser Zeit gut forschen und verwirklichen möchte. Ich hatte ein paar Leute auf der Warteliste, nur um zu wissen, was 1220 bedeutete und es stellte sich heraus, dass sie den Schnitt nicht gemacht haben. Also habe ich nichts verloren und ich weiß, dass 1220 immer noch geschützt ist.

# Capítulo #10 No soy médico soy médico, soy médico científico

Mi razón para escribir este libro es para demostrar que tengo lo que se necesita sin la escuela de medicina. Mis prácticas científicas son equivalentes a un doctorado en medicina. No soy médico, soy doctor científico en evolución humana. Hay múltiples problemas con la Humanidad que estoy abordando a los humanos para ser de hecho. No conseguimos encontrar tu ubicación exacta. Soy un científico de alto secreto que me especializo en muchas áreas diferentes de la ciencia. Probablemente sería uno de los mejores médicos si estudiara esa forma de ir. Permítanme que se sepa que aprecio a los buenos médicos que trabajan en el Hospital realizando tareas médicas desde cirugías hasta chequeos. Lo que tengo que traer a la mesa está más allá de eso. Todo el mundo no escucha buenas noticias, lo que les ayudará, etc. Eso no significa que no sean conscientes. Diré que la mayoría de los problemas se pueden resolver y El Planeta puede estar en su curso en una dirección diferente más beneficiosa para la Humanidad. Tomo mi Pr Científica ... Operaciones para ayudar en El Mundo que no son dañinas para los seres humanos. 1220 Sociedad Científica Soy Comandante y Jefe todas las prácticas son sensibles así que soy yo en el exterior mirando hacia adentro. Llegué a un nivel que me hizo uno y millones en todas las comunidades de la Sociedad Científica con 7.000 millones de personas en El Mundo sólo 700.000 personas tienen el potencial. Podrían estar vivos o muertos para ser exactos. Especialmente cuando una mayoría científica de la gente en El Mundo está cerrada de mente, ni siquiera quieren aprender y luego continuar prefieren dejar pasar la oportunidad. No sólo decir que la Sociedad Científica 1220 tiene 80 años para reinar de 2020 a 2100. Es una bendición que quiero hacer un montón de buena investigación & documentación sucede en ese tiempo. Tenía algunas personas en la lista de espera sólo para saber lo que 1220 significaba y resultó que no hicieron el corte. Así que no perdí nada y sé que 1220 sigue protegido.

# 第#11章
# 不要死於過量

　　僅僅因為我是一個醫生和科學家與我自己的科學協會，並不意味著我不明白。從小到大，我過去常看不起某些藥物。當我長大了，我經歷了一些和更多的藥物，我永遠不會這樣做。我從紐約的舍內塔迪大學度假去了科羅拉多。在我離開紐約之前，我唯一使用的藥物是大麻、迷魂藥、莫莉、酸和酒精。當我到達科羅拉多后不久，可卡因是免費的。我沒有得到它所有的時間，但當我這樣做，它通常是黨。為了快速總結，在科羅拉多州，我使用海洛因，甲烷，裂紋，蘑菇等，如果我不記得。我不是那樣的藥

丸爆裂器，

遠離英雄。我解釋我之所以這麼做，是因為我希望那些過去明白我不只是說話的人。我從來沒有認為自己是一個癮君子，因為我吸毒體驗高：我沒有吸毒，

因為我需要高。我不會危害任何重要的背後使用藥物。作為科學家，藥物不是進口的...

# Kapitel #11 Nicht an einer Überdosis sterben

Nur weil ich ein Arzt & ein Wissenschaftler mit meiner eigenen wissenschaftlichen Gesellschaft bin, bedeutet das nicht, dass ich es nicht verstehe. Aufgewachsen, benutze ich, um auf bestimmte Drogen zu schauen. Als ich älter wurde, erlebte ich einige und mehr Drogen, die ich nie gemacht hätte. Ich ging nach Colorado auf einem College-Urlaub von Schenectady, N.Y. Bevor ich New York verließ, waren die einzigen Drogen, die ich benutzte, Marihuana, Ecstasy, Molly, Acid und Alkohol. Als ich nach Colorado kam, war Kokain nicht kurz nachdem Kokain frei war. Ich habe es nicht die ganze Zeit bekommen, aber als ich es tat, war es in der Regel zu feiern. Um es schnell zusammenzufassen, in Colorado benutze ich Kokain, Meth, Crack, Pilze usw., wenn ich mich nicht erinnern kann. Ich war kein Pillen-Popper wie dieser und blieb heroine fern. Der Grund, warum ich erklärt habe, was ich getan habe, ist, weil ich will, dass Leute, die verstehen, dass ich nicht nur rede. Ich habe mich nie für einen Süchtigen gehalten, weil ich Drogen gemacht habe, um das Rauschzuerleben zu erfahren; Ich habe keine Drogen genommen, weil ich hoch sein musste. Ich würde nichts Wichtiges hinter dem Drogenkonsum aufs Spiel setzen. Als Wissenschaftler sind Medikamente nicht importiert ...

# Capítulo #11 No mueras por una sobredosis

Sólo porque sea doctor y científico de mi propia Sociedad Científica, no significa que no lo entienda. Al crecer, solía mirar hacia abajo en ciertas drogas. Cuando crecí experimenté algunas y más drogas que nunca habría hecho. Fui a Colorado de vacaciones universitarias desde Schenectady, Nueva York. Antes de salir de Nueva York las únicas drogas que usé eran marihuana, éxtasis, molly, ácido y alcohol. Cuando llegué a Colorado no poco después de que la cocaína estuviera libre. No lo conseguí todo el tiempo, pero cuando lo hice normalmente era de fiesta. Para resumirlo rápido, en Colorado uso cocaína, metanfetaminas, crack, setas, etc. si no puedo recordar. No era un reventador de píldoras así *y me alejé de Heroine. La razón por la que explíqué lo que hice es porque quiero que la gente que usa entienda que no sólo estoy hablando. Nunca me consideré un adicto porque hice drogas para experimentar lo alto; No tomé drogas porque necesitaba estar drogado. No pondría en peligro nada importante detrás del uso de drogas. Como un científico medicamentos no son de importación ...*

# 第#12章
# 瞭解你的身體

　　作為人，有時我們認為生活是理所當然的。我曾經是"作為人"的一部分，這就是為什麼我這樣說。現在，通過研究和學習我的知識，我學到了更多。我知道不瞭解你的身體會給自己造成傷害。所以要明白你的身體是面向閱讀觀眾和一般人。現在說"瞭解你的身體"注意細節，你必須擔心你人類存在的每一個元素。沒有得到適當的休息會影響你未來的運作方式。我想談談身體是如何工作的，以及如何保持它的工作。隨著時間的推移，你會聽到一些關於增強免疫系統的事情。聽到這麼多，你認為有沒有別的促進是的，有。我可能會寫一個醫生的做法，提供主題和必要的資訊，但我會離開它開放給你做進一步的研究。當然，在人體中還有其他的東西可以促進，這會讓你瞭解你的身體。...

# Kapitel #12
# Verstehen Sie Ihren Körper

Als Menschen nehmen wir das Leben manchmal als selbstverständlich hin. Ich benutze, ein Teil von "Als Menschen" zu sein, deshalb habe ich das gesagt. Mit meinem Wissen aus Forschung und Studium habe ich nun mehr gelernt. Ich bin mir des Schadens bewusst, den ich mir zufügen würde, wenn ich deinen Körper nicht verstehe. Verstehen Sie also, dass Ihr Körper auf das Lesepublikum und die Menschen im Allgemeinen ausgerichtet ist. Jetzt sagen "Verstehen Sie Ihren Körper" unter Beachtung der Besonderheiten, müssen Sie sich um jedes Element Ihrer menschlichen Existenz kümmern. Nicht die richtige Ruhe kann beeinflussen, wie Sie in der Zukunft arbeiten. Ich möchte darüber sprechen, wie der

Körper arbeitet und wie er funktioniert. Im Laufe der Zeit hören Sie Dinge über die Stärkung Ihres Immunsystems. Wenn man hört, dass man so viel zu hören glaubt, dass es nichts anderes gibt, um ja zu steigern, gibt es. Ich schreibe vielleicht eine Arztpraxis, die Themen und notwendige Informationen liefert, aber ich werde es offen lassen, damit Sie weitere Forschung enden können. Natürlich gibt es andere Dinge, um im menschlichen Körper zu steigern, die Ihnen erlauben, Ihren Körper zu verstehen. ...

# Capítulo #12
# Entender tu cuerpo

Como personas a veces damos la vida por sentada. Yo solía ser parte de "Como gente" por eso dije eso. Ahora, con mis conocimientos de investigación y estudio aprendí más. Soy consciente del daño que me pondría al no entender tu cuerpo. Así que entiende que tu cuerpo está orientado hacia el público lector y la gente en general. Ahora que dice "Entiende tu cuerpo" prestando atención a los detalles, tienes que preocuparte por cada elemento de tu existencia humana. No obtener el descanso adecuado puede afectar la forma en que opera en el futuro. Quiero hablar sobre cómo funciona el cuerpo y cómo mantenerlo funcionando. En el transcurso del tiempo escuchas cosas sobre cómo estimular tu sistema inmunitario. Oyendo tanto crees que no hay nada más que aumentar sí hay. Tal vez escribo una práctica del Doctor proporcionando temas e información necesaria pero voy a dejarla abierta para que hagas más investigaciones. Por supuesto, hay otras cosas para impulsar en el cuerpo humano que le permitirá entender su cuerpo. ...

# 第#13章
# 如何照顧自己，如何對待他人

　　**既然我**說的是如何照顧自己，我不得不說"**我必須做好**"。**我是人類進化的科學博士：我在不同的層面上處理這個世界。這不僅對我來**說是必不可少的，以確保我是乾淨的，有食物吃。我基本上必須繼續學習和研究，所以我不是在黑暗的精神。從我年輕的時候起，我就知道我必須繼續學習。作為一個梅森與試圖把人帶進來或放棄秘密知識無關。我很高興我是梅森照顧好自己 360°

**我不指望人們能理解。我如何照顧自**

己，正在尋求。在《世界》中，
我能描述的對待別人的最好方式就是表示尊重，
確保人們瞭解我是誰。我寧願和沒有問題的人打交道，因為我是醫生，我寧願治癒也不願做別的事情。我給人們所需要的機會，無論他們是否接受。沒人會告訴你...

# Kapitel #13 Wie man sich um mich selbst kümmert und wie man mit anderen umgeht

Da ich darüber spreche, wie ich mich um mich selbst kümmere, muss ich sagen: "Ich muss einen guten Job machen". Ich bin ein wissenschaftlicher Doktor der menschlichen Evolution; Ich beschäftige mich mit dieser Welt auf einer anderen Ebene. Es ist nicht nur wichtig für mich, um sicherzustellen, dass ich sauber bin und Essen zu essen. Ich muss im Grunde weiter studieren und forschen, damit ich mental nicht im Dunkeln bin. Da ich jünger war ein rechter und genauer Mason, wusste ich, dass ich mit meinem Studium weitermachen musste. Mason zu sein hat nichts damit zu tun, Menschen hereinzubringen oder das geheime Wissen zu verschenken. Ich bin glücklich, dass ich ein Mason bin. Sich um mich selbst zu kümmern 360° und ich erwarte nicht, dass die Leute verstehen. Wie ich mich um mich selbst kümmere, sucht. Der beste Weg in The World, den ich beschreiben kann, wenn man andere Menschen behandelt, ist Respekt zu zeigen und sicherzustellen, dass die Menschen verstehen, wer ich bin. Ich beschäme mich lieber mit Menschen ohne Probleme, weil ich ein Arzt bin, den ich eher heile, als etwas anderes zu tun. Ich gebe den Menschen die Möglichkeit, die sie brauchen, ob sie es ergreifen oder nicht. Niemand wird yo sagen ...

# Capítulo #13 Cómo cuidarme y cómo tratar a los demás

Ya que estoy hablando de cómo cuidar de mí mismo, tengo que decir "tengo que hacer un buen trabajo". Soy doctor científico en evolución humana; Estoy tratando con este Mundo a un nivel diferente. No es sólo esencial para mí para asegurarse de que estoy limpio y tengo comida para comer. Básicamente tengo que seguir estudiando e investigando para no estar en la oscuridad mentalmente. Desde que era más joven un derecho & exacto Mason, sabía que tenía que seguir adelante con mis estudios. Ser albañil no tiene nada que ver con tratar de traer a la gente o regalar El conocimiento secreto. Estoy feliz de ser un Mason. Cuidarme 360° y no espero que la gente lo entienda. Cómo me cuido, es buscar. La mejor manera en El Mundo que puedo describir tratando a otras personas es mostrando respeto, asegurándome de que la gente entienda quién soy. Prefiero tratar con gente sin ningún problema porque soy un Doctor que prefiero curar que hacer otra cosa. Le doy a la gente la oportunidad que necesitan, lo tomen o no. Nadie te lo va a decir...

# 第#14章
# 選擇健康而不是樂趣

　　這是一個重要的話題，因為人們不會清楚地看到它。在這一章中，我不會告訴你，
你必須是一個健康垃圾或類似的東西。我只是解釋選擇健康而不是樂趣，所以我們都知道我們的極限，不管我們是否克服它們。在這個描述中，我指出要注意你的健康。有些人依靠物質來通過或他們最喜歡的食物，這可能是破壞性的。選擇健康而不是樂趣，把你的健康放在奢侈品之前，無論是對健康造成損害的活動，還

是對健康造成損害的食物。我要舉幾個例子：如果舉重導致健康問題，比如影響你的心臟，是時候改變你的鍛煉方式了。這是選擇健康而不是樂趣，因為鍛煉會很有趣，如果你到了這一點。食物的一個例子就像服用能提高血壓、高膽固醇、引發糖尿病、肝衰竭、腎臟問題等的食物。喬西...

# Kapitel #14 Wählen Sie Gesundheit über Spaß

Das ist ein wichtiges Thema, weil die Leute es nicht klar sehen würden. In diesem Kapitel werde ich Ihnen nicht sagen, Sie müssen ein Gesundheits-Junky oder so etwas sein. Ich erkläre einfach, gesundheit statt Spaß zu wählen, also kennen wir alle unsere Grenzen, ob wir sie überschreiten oder nicht. In dieser Beschreibung weise ich darauf hin, achten Sie auf Ihre Gesundheit. Es gibt Menschen, die auf Substanzen angewiesen sind, um sie durchzubringen, oder ihr Lieblingsfutter, das zerstörerisch sein kann. Wählen Sie Gesundheit über Spaß stellen Sie Ihre Gesundheit vor Luxus, ob es eine Aktivität verursacht Schäden an Ihrer Gesundheit oder ein Lebensmittel verursacht

Schäden an Ihrer Gesundheit. Ich werde ein paar Beispiele nennen: Wenn das Heben von Gewichten gesundheitliche Probleme verursacht, wie z. B. ihr Herz zu beeinträchtigen, ist es an der Zeit, die Art und Weise, wie Sie trainieren, umzuschalten. Das ist die Wahl der Gesundheit über Spaß, weil das Training würde Spaß machen, wenn Sie an diesen Punkt zu bekommen. Ein Beispiel für Lebensmittel wäre wie bei der Einnahme von Lebensmitteln, die Ihren Blutdruck erhöht, hohe Cholesterinwerte, Bildung von Diabetes, Leberversagen, Nierenprobleme usw. Choosi ...

# Capítulo #14 Elige la salud antes que la diversión

Este es un tema importante porque la gente no lo vería claramente. En este capítulo no te voy a decir que tienes que ser un adicto a la salud o algo así. Simplemente estoy explicando la salud sobre la diversión, para que todos conozcamos nuestros límites, ya sea que los superemos o no. En esta descripción estoy señalando prestar atención a su salud. Hay personas que dependen de sustancias para conseguir a través de ellos o su comida favorita, que puede ser destructivo. Elija salud sobre diversión ponga su salud antes de lujo si se trata de una actividad que causa daños a su salud o un alimento que causa daños a su salud. Voy a dar algunos ejemplos: Si levantar pesas está causando problemas de salud como afectar tu corazón es hora de cambiar la forma en que haces ejercicio. Eso es elegir la salud por encima de la diversión porque hacer ejercicio sería divertido si llegaras a ese punto. Un ejemplo para los alimentos sería como tomar alimentos que aumentan la presión arterial, colesterol alto, crear diabetes, insuficiencia hepática, problemas renales, etc. Choosi ...

# 第#15章
# 我為什麼要用避孕套

　　這樣的對話是主要的，必須表達出來。我為什麼要用避孕套？這對男性和女性在人類中都起著重要作用。如果你看看陰莖，我們只考慮它的兩個放電。我們觀察陰莖以排出精子和尿液。也可以有其他的放電，這將需要我更多的研究來弄清楚。我可以說即使避孕套不是100%能夠保護你在時，除了它可以打破的百分比，這需要小心注意。感染和疾病的傳播是真實的。我敢肯定，所有的人或大多數人都知道這些事情。婦女應該通過讓男人在時使用避孕套來保護自己，因為男性可以向女性傳播疾病，這是很常見的。我有一個甜蜜的一面，女性，所以知道一個男人可以讓一個女人進入她的情緒只是為了讓她懷孕或不關心和傳播疾病。女性有很多擔心處理她的陰道,
所以避孕套應該是...

# Kapitel #15 Warum ich ein Kondom verwenden sollte

Ein Gespräch wie dieses ist groß und muss zum Ausdruck gebracht werden. Warum sollte ich ein Kondom verwenden? Dies spielt eine wichtige Rolle in der Menschheit für Männlich & Weiblich. Wenn Sie sich den Penis anschauen, denken wir nur an seine zwei Entladungen. Wir schauen auf den Penis, um Sperma und Urin zu entladen. Es kann auch andere Entlastungen geben, die mich mehr studieren würde, um herauszufinden. Ich kann sagen "Auch wenn ein Kondom nicht 100% in der Lage ist, Sie während des Geschlechtsverkehrs zu schützen" abgesehen von dem Prozentsatz, dass es brechen kann, muss dies sorgfältig beachtet werden. Die Ausbreitung von Infektionen und

Krankheiten ist real. Ich bin mir ziemlich sicher, dass alle Leute oder meistens alle Leute über diese Dinge Bescheid wissen. Frauen sollten sich schützen, indem sie einen Mann dazu bringen, ein Kondom beim Sex zu verwenden, weil Männchen Krankheiten auf Frauen ausbreiten können, was häufig ist. Ich habe eine süße Seite für Frauen, also weiß, dass ein Mann ein Weibchen in ihre Emotionen bekommen kann, nur um sie schwanger zu machen oder sich nicht zu kümmern und eine Krankheit zu verbreiten. Eine Frau hat eine Menge zu kümmern über den Umgang mit ihrer Vagina, so dass ein Kondom sollte die ...

# Capítulo #15 Por qué debería usar un condón

Una conversación como esta es importante y debe expresarse. ¿Por qué debería usar un condón? Esto juega un papel importante en la Humanidad tanto para hombres como para mujeres. Si nos fijamos en el pene sólo pensamos en sus dos descargas. Miramos el pene para descargar espermatozoides y orina. También puede haber otras descargas, lo que me llevaría más estudiar para averiguarlo. Puedo decir "Incluso si un condón no es 100% capaz de protegerte durante las relaciones sexuales" aparte del porcentaje que puede romper, esto debe ser cuidadosamente prestado atención a. La propagación de infecciones y enfermedades es real. Estoy bastante seguro de que toda la gente o sobre todo toda la gente sabe de estas cosas. Las mujeres deben protegerse haciendo que un hombre use un condón durante el sexo porque los hombres pueden propagar enfermedades a las mujeres, lo cual es común. Tengo un lado dulce para las mujeres, así que sé que un hombre puede meter a una hembra en sus emociones sólo para embarazarla o no cuidarla y propagar una enfermedad. Una hembra tiene mucho de qué preocuparse con lidiar con su vagina por lo que un condón debe ser el ...

# 章#16我可以有一個以上的醫生

　　我介紹了這本書關於幫助人們。我不希望它是對其他醫生的偏見。我希望另一個醫生也能閱讀和欣賞我的書。我知道我可以有更多的醫生。我有一個非常好的關係，我的眼科醫生在博爾德科羅拉多州&我作為病人。在我訪問那裡期間，我們非常關心彼此，並參與智力對話。他對我來說是最好的：即使他們在工作，也一點也不像在專業人士身邊。我很感激;我也喜歡醫生的我和病人醫生有一些最好的關係。即使醫生是醫生，如果他們知道他們在做什麼，這是偉大的。我可以有不止一個醫生

，　這不僅僅是關於我的經驗，
它是關於看它以不同的方式和欣賞你
的醫生的。

# Kapitel #16 ich kann mehr als einen Arzt haben

Ich habe dieses Buch in Bezug auf die Hilfe für Menschen vorgestellt. Ich möchte nicht, dass es eine Voreingenommenheit gegenüber anderen Doktor enden wird. Ich hoffe, dass auch ein anderer Arzt mein Buch lesen und schätzen kann. Ich weiß, dass ich mehr haben kann als auf Doktor. Ich habe eine sehr schöne Beziehung zu meinem Augenarzt in Boulder Colorado & mir als Patient. Uns ist es sehr wichtig, uns zu sehen und während meiner Besuche dort in intellektuelle Gespräche zu kommen. Er ist der Beste für mich; es ist nichts wie um einen Profi zu sein, auch wenn sie bei der Arbeit sind. Ich weiß das zu schätzen; Ich liebe auch Medical Doctor's. Ich hatte einige der besten

Beziehungen mit Patienten Arztbesuche. Auch wenn ein Arzt ein Arzt ist, wenn sie wissen, was sie tun, ist es großartig. Ich kann mehr als einen Doktor haben, es geht nicht nur um meine Erfahrungen, es geht darum, es anders zu betrachten und deinen Doktor zu schätzen.

# Capítulo #16 puedo tener más de un Doctor

Presenté este libro con respecto a ayudar a la gente. No quiero que sea un sesgo hacia otro Doctor. Espero que incluso otro Doctor pueda leer y apreciar mi libro. Sé que puedo tener más que en doctor. Tengo una relación muy agradable con mi Eye Doctor en Boulder Colorado y conmigo como paciente. Realmente nos preocupamos por vernos y entrar en conversaciones intelectuales a lo largo de mis visitas allí. Él es el mejor para mí; no se parece en nada a estar cerca de un profesional, incluso si están en el trabajo. Te lo agradezco; También me encanta doctor médico. Tuve algunas de las mejores relaciones con el paciente Doctor Visits. A pesar de que un Doctor es un Doctor, si saben lo que están haciendo es genial. Puedo tener más de un Doctor, no se trata sólo de mis experiencias, se trata de mirarlo de una manera diferente y apreciar a su Médico.

# 第#17章
# 不要讓痛苦持續太久

　　這一章是基於照顧你，在事情變得更糟之前。當你發現自己經歷疼痛或不尋常的事情時，去看專科醫生。事情可以根據對櫃檯藥物的常識來治療。還有一些事情需要處理，因為沒有別的辦法。人體經歷它成長的經歷，它變老，變年輕，它死去。當我談論它死了，我指的是你還活著，事情順其自然。當你剪指甲，你的頭髮，或者你得到一個削減，廢料或只是皮膚脫落死亡。然後身體恢復活力，這些東西又長回來了。我指的是皮膚

的新生長，
無論什麼階段和年齡變老，
至少我沒有在我的科學社會。不要感
到疼痛，只是忍受它而不尋求救濟，
通過接受治療。照顧你是一種責任。

# Kapitel #17 Lassen Sie den Schmerz nicht zu lange an

Dieses Kapitel basiert darauf, sich um sie zu kümmern, bevor sich die Dinge verschlimmern. Wenn Sie sich durch Schmerzen oder etwas außergewöhnliches gehen, gehen Sie einen Spezialisten auf. Thing es kann nach allgemeinem Wissen von über den Gegenden Medikamente behandelt werden. Dann gibt es noch andere Dinge, die behandelt werden müssen, weil es keinen anderen Weg gibt. Der menschliche Körper durchlebt Erfahrungen, er wird alt, er wird jünger, und er stirbt. Wenn ich darüber spreche, stirbt ich davon, dass du noch am Leben bist und die Dinge seinen Lauf nehmen. Wenn Sie Ihre Fingernägel schneiden, Ihr Haar, oder Sie bekommen einen Schnitt,

Schrott oder nur Haut fallen von ihm stirbt. Dann verjüngt sich der Körper und diese Dinge werden wieder angebaut. Ich beziehe mich auf das neue Wachstum der Haut, egal in welchem Stadium und Alter, dass ich nicht älter werde, zumindest nicht in meiner Wissenschaftlichen Gesellschaft. Fühlen Sie keine Schmerzen und dulden Sie es einfach, ohne Hilfe zu suchen, indem Sie behandelt werden. Es ist eine Pflicht, sich um Sie zu kümmern.

# Capítulo #17 No dejes que el dolor se mantenga por mucho tiempo

Este capítulo se basa en cuidar de ti, antes de que las cosas empeoren. Cuando te encuentres pasando por el dolor o algo fuera de lo común, ve a ver a un especialista. Las cosas se pueden tratar de acuerdo con el conocimiento común de medicamentos de venta libre. Luego hay otras cosas que necesitan ser tratadas porque no hay otra manera. El cuerpo humano pasa por experiencias que crece, envejece, se hace más joven y muere. Cuando estoy hablando de que muere me refiero a que sigues vivo y las cosas siguen su curso. Cuando te cortas las uñas de los dedos, tu cabello o te cortan, raspas o simplemente la piel se cae de él muere. Entonces el cuerpo se rejuvenece y esas cosas se vuelven a cultivar. Me refiero al nuevo crecimiento de la piel sin importar la etapa y la edad como envejecer al menos no lo hago en mi Sociedad Científica. No sientas dolor y simplemente lo toleres sin buscar alivio a través de recibir tratamiento. Es un deber cuidar de ti.

# 第#18章不要在長袍外面評判我

　　人們希望看到一些能展示他們所想的東西，以尋求安慰。在這個世界上，很多事情被誤解了，沒有因為缺乏歸屬感而得到讚揚。我寫了這篇文章，做了一個明確的聲明。不要在長袍外面評判我。我說的是我的醫生長袍我是一個真正的醫生不只是使用標題，

**使自己必須在一個類別沒有生**產。有許多醫生在那裡誰贏得了冠軍，有些人只是去的標題，不能做的工作。我是一名醫生，因為我關心治愈人們建立我的科學實踐作為一種形式的健康的人和我自己。我不應該穿長袍不被

評判。由於我能夠寫我的醫生實踐，這並沒有把我從我的科學秘密分開，只是使一個前站在我感到快樂和行為。我計劃超越這本書和人類所知道的一切。我的意圖有一天是。開一家醫院招聘護士來説明我...

# Kapitel #18 Richte mich nicht außerhalb meiner Robe

Die Menschen möchten etwas sehen, das das darstellt, was sie von etwas zur Beruhigung halten. In dieser Welt werden viele Dinge missverstanden und nicht wegen der mangelnden Zugehörigkeit gewürdigt. Ich habe mit dem Schreiben eine klare Erklärung abgegeben. Richten Sie mich nicht außerhalb meiner Robe. Die Robe, von der ich spreche, ist meine Doktorrobe. Ich bin ein echter Doktor, der nicht nur den Titel benutzt, um mich in einer Kategorie ohne Produktion zu machen. Es gibt viele Ärzte da draußen, die den Titel verdienen und einige, die nur durch den Titel gehen und die Arbeit nicht tun können. Ich bin Ein Arzt, weil es mir wichtig ist, Menschen zu heilen, die meine wissenschaftlichen

Praktiken als eine Form der Gesundheit für Menschen und mich selbst etablieren. Ich sollte kein Gewand tragen müssen, um nicht beurteilt zu werden. Da ich in der Lage bin, meine Doktorpraxis zu schreiben, die mich nicht von meinen wissenschaftlichen Geheimnissen trennt, macht nur einen ehemaligen Stand für mich glücklich und dirigieren. Ich plane, über dieses Buch und alles, was der Menschheit bekannt ist, hinauszugehen. Meine Absichten eines Tages sind. Ein Krankenhaus zu eröffnen, das Krankenschwestern rekrutiert, um mir zu helfen c ...

# Capítulo #18 No me juzgues fuera de mi túnica

A la gente le gustaría ver algo que presente lo que piensan de algo para tranquilizarse. En este mundo muchas cosas son malinterpretadas y no se les da crédito por la falta de pertenencia. Hice una declaración clara con la escritura de esto. No me juzgues fuera de mi bata. La túnica de la que hablo es mi bata de doctor. Soy un verdadero doctor no sólo usando el título para hacerme tener que estar en una categoría de no producción. Hay muchos médicos por ahí que ganan el título y algunos que simplemente van por el título y no pueden hacer el trabajo. Soy médico porque me importa curar a la gente estableciendo mis prácticas científicas como una forma de salud para las personas y para mí. No debería tener que usar una túnica para no ser juzgado. Como soy capaz de escribir mi consultorio médico, que no me separa de mis secretos científicos sólo hace que un antiguo que representa para mí para sentirse feliz & conducta. Planeo ir más allá de este libro y todo lo conocido por la humanidad. Mis intenciones algún día son. Para abrir un hospital reclutando enfermeras para ayudarme c ...

# West Coast Gang Counselor

I am a West Coast Gang Counselor, I help people in Gangs change their lives, so they don't have to go down the wrong road. I work with different employers, and try to get them to establish long term work history, so they can see another way of living, other than just wasting time. I started in Colorado just getting involved, showing them I care. It's not hard for me to get through to them; I hope this book helps me open up more opportunity for them. There are a lot of them out there doing well, working with them has never felt, less than great.

-West Coast Gang Counselor: Jaheem R.Hilts-

## ABOUT THE AUTHOR

I'm Jaheem, I'm very professional. I'm from America, North America.
I consider myself to be lucky, being born in New York State,Schenectady, New York.
Growing up, I didn't see opportunity the way I do now as an Adult.In my life as a Mason,
I have been around a lot of professionals, with different backgrounds. I feel blessed
to have my own Scientific Society, 1220 leading in the World. I plan to help people,
and continue to do what I know is right.

### ABOUT THE BOOK

This is book is a presentation, a Scientific practice, which is showing
how it is equivalent to a Doctor of Medicine Degree. This is for professionals,
like Scientist and Doctors or anyone else that may want to see between these pages.

## Energy Massacre

**Scientist Doctor of Human Evolution:**

**Scientist: Jaheem R.Hilts**

## Scientific Doctor

**Energy bashes continuously surging rapidly unfelt. Through windows with no curtains, trapped in elements that rupture, out of dimensions never known to Mankind. As you embrace the pain of no pain, understanding its hard to achieve, dying and living over and over, the energy still remains.**

**1220 Sci-Society**

1220

*Scientific Society*

*1220 Scientific Society Founder*
*Jaheem R.Hilts*

*Scientist of Human Evolution*
*Scientific Doctor of Human Evolution*
*Doctor of Medicine*
*Scholar= Jaheem Rashon Hilts*

*You can't find Wisdom if your lost. If Wisdom can't find you it must be lost. I am a Angel in The Flesh, a blessing in disguise a King about The Earth. I stand alone as we fight together. If all Hell broke loose, where would you be headed? If I take myself serious? Love can cut and cut & cut until there is nothing there except the pieces of flesh that were cut by Love. I fight the losing battle and gain victory in shadow. My Honor wishes I wasn't born. From: Adam to King Solomon I have grown not to part............*

*By: Jaheem R.Hilts*
*1220 Sci-Soc Report*

# Location Operation 3.7

1220
Scientific Society
Certified Scientific Doctor
<u>Jaheem R.Hilts</u>

*When your mouth is closed and your eyes are open... 1220 (Sci-Soc) report*

When existence becomes more of a opportunity, we start to comprehend what we missed. With the right point the exceleration of knowledge is a profound youth for the nuturing. This location is Top Secret which everything is Top Secret at all times in life. There are a mass amount of things the World population is not ready to accept. The Secret is more than a comfort zone.

The Illuminati King
King Illuminati= Jaheem R.Hilts

@Nothing Plays a major part
Scientific Doctor of Human Evolution:
Scientific Doctor= Jaheem R.Hilts

3-7-13-23-12-20-14

From: precious stones that i don't own, to The Throne I am. a continuation of Love undegrading. The master Plan- Host of The Event. I am The Science of all (?). my (?) would of made me Illuminati King at birth, since I can live up to it, I became myself. I'm not just all that you know, I'm a Top Secret Scientific Doctor in different Dimensions, in a World full of ignorant people claiming to know something. all I want to do is me. Shout out to The 1220 Scientific Society I'm The Founder of, Commando & Chief.
   Documentation World Science Report: Global 4:30pm (MT) Sci-Soc

# The New World Order 2009

1220
Scientific Society

## Triangle over The Circle

Scientific Doctor of Human Evolution=
Scientific Doctor= NWO Jaheem R.Hilts

(Building Practice)

Doctor of Medicine
Jaheem R.Hilts

Let me set the tone straight. There is no need to fear The New World Order, it is something that happens for the good of Humanity, to service all of The World.Some see it as a negative opportunity, its really ironing out the distance from full industrial agriculture & less crime Worldwide. Crime should not be the main source of highlighted information, by news outlets. There is a power struggle to keep peace, with The New World Order that would be established.Does it mean everybody will have the same power no, it does mean all would be equal in the eyes of each individual.What matters Matters and what doesn't doesn't. Don't be fooled.The New World Order is Peace, on Earth.

## CAN YOU REALLY WAKE UP? IS THERE A ANSWER NOT FULLY EXPRESSED? IS THERE A MISTAKE? HOW DO YOU MEASURE (?) AND THEN FORGET THERE IS NO (?)

The Spiritual Attack that brings living again
Scientific Doctor of Human Evolution
Scientific Doctor= Jaheem R.Hilts

Being in awe is traumatizing more than losing yourself and finding a better way of not being you. Here at 1220 Scientific Society we are Mechanics of fixing The Soul hoping not to cause a issue between The Mind and Spirit. There is no free offer when spending time to make a choice costs. Welcome to Reality.

1220 Sci-Soc

**Scientist Doctor of Human Evolution:**
Scientist-Jaheem R.Hilts
1220
Scientific Society

People have become their own victims to their decision making, then not understanding how they did it. Their is more of a problem, how can you be against what makes you fulfilled, what makes you whole? There is no reason why things are easy, then made difficult as if The World is designed not to be heard. The only joke is a waste of life then regrets. At what point is it legit to realize? Life is different than ability, life is not on terms with just exisiting.
By: 1220 Scientist Jaheem R.Hilts (Society)

# The Earth is a madhouse

-A brief Scientific discussion/topic-

1220
Scientific Society
By: Scientific Doctor of Human Evolution
Scientific Doctor= Jaheem R·Hilts

(1220 Sci-Soc)

Ignorance is deeper than what we identify it as, people shift through The World trying to make sense of ordinary things, from choices to behavior· How can life be so simple and not so simple? In The World today we are up against not just people having a bad day but we are up against people finding happiness in ignorance· Wisdom chases wisdom· A house without a foundation is a madhouse· Which dealing with people sometimes is mad·

*Scientific Doctor= Jaheem R.Hilts*

## (Complete nurture & Salvation)
## Scientific will & ways

*My Heart has broken from the pressures of The world. I don't stand hurt, I realize in the process. I don't forget what I want. Now that my heart has come to a length of understanding, it swallows only the necessary to keep me elevated. Believe in me, it's a Faith waiting to be cherished......1220 (sci)*

## Scientific Doctor Machine

-Gravity Upside- - Down-

King Illuminati= Jaheem R.Hilts

1220

## Scientific Society Founder
Exquisite, Esteem, Honor

Bursting into existence losing consciousness gaining in multiplicity. Raging through unknown identification, breaking off becoming new. Leaving creation back and forth, producing similar results not in the same way. Reflecting in circumference lost still existing, stronger than awareness, close to Eternity.

Nov. 20th, 2020 (1220 Sci-Soc)

# HOLY CERTIFIED
## SCHOLARHOOD

### SCIENTIFIC DOCTOR OF HUMAN EVOLUTION..............

SCIENTIFIC DOCTOR= JAHEEM R.HILTS
1220 SCIENTIFIC SOCIETY FOUNDER

I AM A SCHOLAR WITH COMPLETE KNOWLEDGE FAR MORE GREATER THAN WHAT GOD WOULD JUST HAND OVER. I SPECIALIZE IN SPIRITUAL DEVELOPMENT, SECRET RITUALS, SCIENTIFIC DIMENSIONS EXCLUSIVE, HUMANITY, THE UNIVERSE, RELIGION, ALL THINGS PRIVATE IN STUDY, THE IMMACULATE THIRD EYE PROCESS ETC.

1220 SCI-SOC

1220
Scientific Society

{ Award }

December 4th, 2020

Doctor of Medicine
Scientific Practices
Honorable Doctorate "Acknowledgement"
Scientific Community "Pursuit of Happiness"

1220 Scientific Society Founder= Jaheem R.Hilts
Scientific Doctor= Jaheem R.Hilts
Doctor of Medicine= Jaheem R.Hilts

This should go with out speaking, for one who puts his life on the line for The Development of The World and staggering set backs by all sorts of people. This award is not for the accused to know, just for only the one who knows. I Jaheem R.Hilts, will take this award as a promise to The People in The World and help out as I can without causing confusion in 1220 Scientific Society. The Honor is in production, cause, results & satisfaction.

The World is home, then out there we find comfort knowing we are home.

# THE MORNING EARTH SETTLERS

1220
SCIENTIFIC SOCIETY

## SCIENTIST DOCTOR OF HUMAN EVOLUTION:
## SCIENTIST: JAHEEM R.HILTS
## 1220 SCIENTIFIC SOCIETY FOUNDER

Би өөргүйгээр амьдарч чадна

**IN MUCH DESPAIR CONSCIOUSNESS HAS NOT PROVEN ITSELF.SIX EARS POSSSIBLE SEVEN FINDING CALM AND STEADY IN NAUSEOUS ENERGY VIBRATIONS.**

1220-

1220-

1220- SCI-SOCIETY

Elite

Чамд байхгүй гэдгийг би маш их зүйл алдлаа

The Evil Camel

1220

Scientific Society

Scientist Doctor of Human Evolution

Scientist Jaheem R.Hilts

1220 Members serve a purpose

Η φλιοφάνεια είναι μια δόξα που καλόπτεται από δυνάμεις εσκαιρών

Inspiration is a fight, eyes are closed trying to develope whats right and wrong. If life was easy there would be no survival, its a whole mess making sense. The gift should be appreciated it withers away as time goes by without proper handling, still it remains. We are provided not to lose reaching has nothing to do with streching out your arms. In the sky I find myself only by a fraction then I keep looking hoping to pick up the pieces that didn't know each other. One side had another side making something complete it still went through a process. Go for more than luck because all happiness doesn't measure the same................(1220 Sci)Society

Great Masonic Puba Scientist: Jaheem R.Hilts

(1220 Scientific Society Founder)

יפה זה יפה

جميل جميل

The beauty of all beauty is beautiful. How can one measure beauty with no knowledge compared to some. Stricken by most things even happiness, which should be evaluated without criticism. The eye that never blinks did not let me down. Transformation was a key, which door did it fit? I lost myself over and over then I discovered something new, it could of been a part if me.

(1220 Sci-Society)

1220
Scientific Society

Lost Mason's Vessel Worship
Planet Earth

Great Puba= Jaheem Rashon Hilts
Scientific Doctor= Jaheem Rashon Marcus
Anthony Hilts (NYS 1986) The US-Inc

This is not for everyone nor is there a desire to compare to the oudsider- We are simple only because we know- I give no graditude to myself ,I am only The Path-

## Mixed Potion
### Secret Society
### 1220
## Scientific Society

Looking deep in yourself is beyond experience. We comprehend the measures as time exceeds over night. The great opportunity is for the student. Much faces a destructive cure. Growth foams decay.
1220 (Sci-Soc) report

By: Scientific Doctor of Human Evolution
Scientific Doctor= Jaheem R.Hilts

The Satanic Pope
The Illuminati Grandson
Great Puba Mason
Slave Master's Grandson
Slave Master Jaheem R.Hilts
King Mason
King Solomon II
Illuminati Monarch
Illuminati Scientist
1220 Scientific Society Founder
Secret Society Operator
Bavarian King Jaheem Rashon Hilts

April 26th, 2021

I am a Pope, a World Pope, conducting things for The Satanic, in all prosperous ways in existence. I developed from a Monarch King reigning in America, in Secret Societies plus public affairs. My life is based on Trust alone, I don't settle for anything other, in the least, I rather not bother. I give every Female in The World many chances to wake up, unless it's just a dead issue. I am blessed to be The God of The Female, and keep The Secret, Secret. There is a long way to go, when people are not humble enough for new direction, or embracing what makes people great, through initiation. My plans are to keep things going, where they need to go.

The Satanic Pope
The Illuminati Grandson
Great Puba Mason
Slave Master's Grandson
Slave Master Jaheem R.Hilts
King Mason
King Solomon II
Illuminati Monarch
Illuminati Scientist
1220 Scientific Society Founder
Secret Society Operator
Bavarian King Jaheem Rashon Hilts

April 26th, 2021

The Satanic Pope
1220 Scientific Society Founder
Bavarian Illuminati Grandson
Jaheem R. Hilts 1986 N.Y.S.

I am a Pope, a World Pope, conducting things for The Satanic, in all prosperous ways in existence. I developed from a Monarch King reigning in America, in Secret Societies plus public affairs. My life is based on Trust alone, I don't settle for anything other, in the least, I rather not bother. I give every Female in The World many chances to wake up, unless it's just a dead issue. I am blessed to be The God of The Female, and keep The Secret, Secret. There is a long way to go, when people are not humble enough for new direction, or embracing what makes people great, through initiation. My plans are to keep things going, where they need to go.

The Satanic Pope
1220 Scientific Society Founder
Bavarian Illuminati Grandson
Jaheem R. Hilts 1986 N.Y.S.

The Satanic Pope
1220 Scientific Society Founder
Bavarian Illuminati Grandson
Jaheem R. Hilts 1986 N.Y.S.

# A REAL WOMAN

A REAL WOMAN IS BASICALLY NOT JUST WHAT THE WORLD WANTS HER TO BE. SHE DOESN'T HAVE TO FLOSS HER INDEPENDENCE BECAUSE IT WAS IMPORTANT TO HER. BOILING DOWN A REAL WOMAN IS THE CONNECTION OF THE HEART. I DON'T BELIEVE MAN AND WOMAN ARE EQUAL BUT THEY EXIST IN THE WORLD TOGETHER. I BELIEVE A WOMAN IS BETTER THAN A MAN THAT'S JUST ME. A REAL WOMAN DOESN'T HAVE TO FLOSS HER CAPABILITIES BECAUSE CAPABILITIES, VISION AND PLANS, ARE THREE DIFFERENT THINGS. IF A REAL WOMAN DOESN'T KNOW CAN SHE TEACH? THESE ARE FACTS THAT CAN'T BE DISPUTED EVEN IF THEY CAN BE ELABORATED ON. A REAL WOMAN IS NOT JUST FAKING IT TO GET BY EVEN WHEN THINGS JUST DON'T MATCH THE TIME, AND CIRCUMSTANCES IN HER LIFE.

The Satanic Pope Jaheem Rashon Hilts 1986 New York State

Printed in the United States
by Baker & Taylor Publisher Services